CÔTE À CÔTE 2

Le français tel qu'on le pense
Eléments de grammaire, de stylistique et de lexicologie

Copyright © 2017 par Virginia Institute Press, une SRL Villa Magna

Tous droits réservés. Aucune partie de ce livre ne peut être reproduite ou utilisée sous quelque forme et par quelque moyen que ce soit, électronique ou mécanique, y compris par la photocopie, l'enregistrement, ou par tout système de stockage d'information et de recherche documentaire, sans l'accord écrit de l'éditeur.

Virginia Institute Press révise tous les ouvrages qu'elle publie afin d'assurer une qualité linguistique. Virginia Institute Press n'est pas responsable des erreurs de contenu dans la présente publication. Toute erreur de contenu éventuellement trouvée dans cette publication relève de la seule responsabilité de son auteur ou de ses auteurs, qui approuvent la version finale de leurs propres travaux. Virginia Institute Press et les auteurs ne sont, en aucune manière, responsables de l'utilisation par le lecteur du contenu de cette publication.

Pour plus d'informations, veuillez contacter :
Virginia Institute Press/Villa Magna, LLC
PO Box 68425
Virginia Beach, VA 23471

ISBN : 978-1-940178-43-1
Première édition
Conception de la couverture par Diren Yardimli

Imprimé aux États-Unis d'Amérique

Copyright © 2017 by Virginia Institute Press, a Villa Magna, LLC company

All rights reserved. No part of this book may be reproduced or utilized in any form or by any means, electronic or mechanical, including photocopying, recording, or by any information storage and retrieval system, without permission in writing from the publisher.

Virginia Institute Press edits all works it publishes for linguistic quality. Virginia Institute Press is not responsible for any content errors found in this publication. Any content errors eventually found in this publication are the sole responsibility of its author or authors, who approve the final version of their own work. Neither Virginia Institute Press nor the author or authors are responsible in any way whatsoever for the reader's use of the contents in this publication.

For information, contact:
Virginia Institute Press/Villa Magna, LLC
PO Box 68425
Virginia Beach, VA 23471

ISBN: 978-1-940178-43-1
First edition
Cover design by Diren Yardimli

Printed in the United States of America

Cette page a été laissée intentionnellement blanche
This page intentionally left blank

Table of Contents

Rationale 11
Introduction en français 15
Objective and Structure of the Book 19
To the student 21
Chapter 1 - The articles 23
    The Basic System 23
    Other typical cases: 28
Chapter 2 - The qualifying adjective 37
    The Values 39
Chapter 3 - The complement of a noun, and the complement of an adjective 51
    I. The complement of a noun 51
    II. The complement of an adjective. 57
Chapter 4 - The pronoun system: Some problematic cases 65
    I. The Interrogative pronouns: 66
    II. The relative pronouns: 68
    III. The demonstrative pronouns 71
Chapter 5 - More about pronouns 77
    I. The personal pronouns: 77
    II. The possessive pronouns: 79
    III. The indefinite pronouns: 81
Chapter 6 - The expression of movement and its verbs semantics and syntax 91
    I. Sémantique: 91
    II. Syntax: 94
Chapter 7 - The Indicative mood and its verb tenses: perspectives and aspects 101
    I. The perspectives and aspects of verbs: 101
    II. The verb tenses: 103
Chapter 8 - The subjunctive mood: hypothesis and subjectivity 115
    I. The obligatory subjunctive: 117
    II. The optional subjunctive: 121
    III. Verb tenses in the subjunctive mood: 123
Chapter 9 - The conditional mood: hypothesis and unreality 131
    Viewing a condition: 131
    Origin of the conditional form: 132
    I. The conditional mood: 133

II. The conditional as a tense of the indicative mood: 135
  III. Alternate means of expressing condition: 136
Chapter 10 - Problematic Semi-auxiliary verbs: devoir, pouvoir, savoir, vouloir, and verb tenses 141
  I. Tenses and variations in meaning: 142
  II. The syntax of the modal verb: 146
Chapter 11 - The active, passive and pronominal voices 151
  I. The active voice: 152
  II. The passive voice: 152
  III. The pronominal voice: 154
  IV. Pronominal verbs can express several types of actions: 156
Chapter 12 - The infinitive mood 165
  I. The infinitive as subject of a verb: 166
  II. The infinitive as object of a verb: 166
  III. The infinitive as object of an adjective: 169
  IV. The infinitive in adverbial phrases: 169
  V. The infinitive replacing a conjugated verb or a whole clause: 170
  VI. The infinitive replacing the imperative mood: 170
  VII. The passive infinitive: 171
  VIII. The past infinitive: 172
  IX. Some infinitives have become full-fledged nouns: 172
Chapter 13 - The present participle and the gerund 179
  I. The present participle: 179
  II. The gerund: 182
Chapter 14 - Some problematic prepositions 189
  I. *FOR* as a preposition of time: 190
  II. *IN* as a time preposition: 193
  III. *IN* as a preposition of manner: 193
  IV. *ABOUT* as a preposition of approximation: 194
  V. *ON* and its various relations 195
  VI. *TO* and its various relations: 195
  VII. Amplification of a preposition: 197
Chapter 15 - The rich and varied world of adverbs 203
  1) Correspondence of adverbs of time: 204
  2) Correspondence adverb/adjective as comparative and superlative words: 205
  3) The equivalents of the English adverb *late*: 205
  4) Double nature and function of some adverbs: 206

> 5) The derivation of adjectives into adverbs: 207
> 6) From adjective to adverb: Expressions of place: 208
> 7) Formation of adverbs ending in --ment:........................... 208
> 8) The adverbs of negation: Types and place........................ 209

Chapter 16 - The syntax of emphasis 217
> I. Repetition in French for plain emphasis............................ 217
> II. Dislocation in French for exclusive emphasis:.................. 218

Glossary of grammatical terms:.. 225
Bibliography:... 233
Other Books by Virginia Institute Press................................... 235

"Arbitrariness is the salvation of the unexplained"

« *L'arbitraire est le refuge de l'inexpliqué* ».

Jacques Bourgeacq

Rationale

For several decades, grammar had practically disappeared from the French language classroom, for the benefit of methodologies whose objective was to promote the student's free expression and self-confidence in communicating in the foreign language. In recent years, however, grammar seems to have made somewhat of a comeback. One of the reasons why grammar had been discarded in the first place was the dictatorial manner in which it was presented: grammar appeared as the accumulation of a vast set of rules to be mandatorily applied, usually without any attempts to explain them. However, learning all those rules did not seem to improve communication skills. So, the pendulum had swayed to the other side. Grammar was out! It soon became evident, however, that without the support of grammar and syntax, the language articulated by learners often became a sort of "creole," a hybrid of the native language and the foreign language (e.g., *Franglais* or *Frenglish*), uttered for the consumption of listeners usually very familiar with both languages, and who had no use for such a strange assemblage: a rather limited public indeed!

If we have given the impression that we insist on correct expression in conveying one's ideas, that is the case. And there is a reason: A language is not only a vehicle for transmitting messages; it is also a critical component of a specific cultural heritage. When two people speak the same language, not only do they exchange ideas at the practical, utilitarian level, but they also engage in an act of cultural ***cohesion*** (a search for unifying characteristics). We may compare this exchange with wearing the logo and colors of our football club at a game. If, for example, I chose to wear a jersey or a cap of the Iowa Hawkeyes showing a different looking bird and colors other than the traditional black and gold, would I ever be welcomed by the fans as one of them? When a stranger speaks our language correctly, even with an accent, he/she will be readily welcomed, for having manifested clearly and appropriately his/her will and capacity to belong, to blend in our cultural environment. *This* is also communication.

In our French language programs, a more nuanced study of grammar has often been reserved for the higher levels in the foreign language curriculum (3rd or 4th year of study, if not for the graduate level). But by then the student has had ample opportunities to "freely" develop faulty habits, which fossilize over time with frequent repetitions (and we know how bad habits tend to stick.) Therefore, the earlier we can cultivate authentic communication, the better. Teachers, therefore, have a task of devising a more stimulating and efficient way of teaching grammar, and it is our intention to help them meet this challenge.

This book is <u>not</u> intended to compete with, or replace any current language methodology. Neither does it claim to develop verbal comprehension skills. Rather, this book explores a dimension of language learning that has been largely overlooked in both the so-called "communicative" methodologies of the past decades, and the earlier traditional teaching of grammar. Those "communicative" methodologies have privileged the receiving end of a message, namely the act of its transmission, while the *expressive* dynamics of the message, i.e. the **conception which underlies its formulation**, has long taken a back seat in our instructional approaches. This book emphasizes ***expression*** as an important element of ***authentic*** communication.

As we well know from experience, each language has its own ways of conveying ideas. There are many differences in the choice of words, grammatical and syntactical structures, imagery, idioms, etc. These differences are often thought of as mere oddities or idiosyncrasies from a source other than our own language. And those who study foreign languages have learned to accept them as they are, not always asking about the ***why*** of these variations, no matter how bizarre they may seem at times. These variations, however, often stem from a ***specific underlying logic*** developed gradually over the distant past and handed down from generation to generation. This logic has determined, and still determines today, the specific formulation of the ideas that each language expresses.

This question of a relationship between language and thought has a long and controversial history. And it is still debated today among linguists. Some consider that there is <u>no</u> connection at all between our thoughts and the way we express them; that variations between languages are purely accidental and arbitrary. They plainly reject any notion that there might be a cause and effect relation between our thoughts and the manner in which we express them. Others, this author included, posit that language, as a **human** activity, cannot be totally mechanical and incidental; and as it stems from rational and affective processes in the mind, language must reflect, at least to some degree and in some manner, a view of our relation to the world.

The fact that most of us are unaware that a specific view is reflected in the way we formulate a message does not mean that such a view is not there. In fact, it often takes the study of another language to make us aware of these occurrences in our own language. The questions of "How?" and "Why?" we communicate the way we do then become relevant. This would seem to validate the importance of a rational foreign language study, one that explores the connection between thought and language.

The following are a few comparative examples to illustrate this connection:

1) When an English-speaker "walks *in* the rain," a French person will walk **under** the rain (***sous** la pluie*). In this situation, while English states a visual perception; the French expresses a deduction: since rain comes from above, we are under...

2) When an American <u>gets</u> **on** the bus, the Frenchman *climbs **up in*** the bus: "Il *<u>monte</u> **dans*** le bus." The American *enters **onto*** a surface, a platform (***on*** the bus); the Frenchman steps ***up into*** a space, a volume (***in*** the bus). Note that "to enter" does not express verticality as does *monter*. [1]

3) The English sentence: ***"He was told that...,"*** is rendered in

---

[1] Even though today, one can at times access a train from a platform level with the train doors, the verb monter (to climb up) still remains for a while yet in the people's cultural memory.

French by ***"On lui a dit que..."*** (Someone told him that...). Where the English language presents this situation from the point of view of the receiver (***He***), the French view it from the sender's angle (***On*** = Someone). Yet the situation is the same for both. Such contrastive formulas abound in English and French.

There is not a right or a wrong way to express language. The simple fact is that ***any given reality possesses a variety of facets***, and to express it, each language selects one of these facets to the exclusion of the others. This is not to say that some language occurrences cannot be arbitrary, i.e. reflecting no specific viewpoint or underlying cultural concept, but rather a sort of natural evolution. For example, gender-neutral nouns in Latin, which in the plural often ended in ***a***, evolved into French (e.g., *datum -> data = des données; arma = des armes*), and blended with feminine singular nouns that also often ended in ***a*** (e.g., *rosa, anima*). The cause of that transfer from the neutral to the feminine gender was essentially accidental, having no relation at all to any rational or logical process.

So, what is the usefulness of this second volume of the Côte à côte series? Why should it be important to understand the significant distinctions in the typical patterns and tendencies that reflect the specific viewpoint of each language? This book is useful because exploring these viewpoints can stimulate the acquisition of the foreign language by adding a ***rational*** dimension to the learning process. It raises the study of a foreign language to its legitimate intellectual level, on par with other liberal arts disciplines, instead of leaving it at the utilitarian level of the typical commercial language school.

This type of linguistic/cultural analysis can appeal to, and find a use among students of earlier levels than senior college or graduate school, and possibly a motivated younger student. Such exploration should stress and lead to ***authentic*** communication. Ultimately, ***real*** communication needs indeed an awareness of a language's own vision and logic. More importantly, this book provides, at the practical level, an incentive to resist the tendency to use the structures of one's native language to communicate in another language.

Introduction en français

Pendant les dernières décennies, l'enseignement de la grammaire française (et d'ailleurs des autres langues étrangères) dans les écoles et les universités américaines avait presque totalement cessé. L'enseignement était basé sur des méthodes dites « communicatives », qui visaient à favoriser chez l'étudiant la confiance en soi en lui permettant d'exprimer librement ses idées dans la langue étrangère. Le bon usage de la grammaire était devenu un obstacle à la libre expression, et elle fut ainsi reléguée aux archives.

Dans l'engouement de ces nouvelles méthodes qui déliaient les langues, il fallut du temps pour s'apercevoir que le langage qui sortait de la bouche de nos élèves n'était ni du français, ni de l'anglais, mais un étrange mélange des deux. Tendance toute normale bien sûr pour qui possède instinctivement les structures de sa langue maternelle, la langue anglaise généreusement contribuait sa syntaxe et ses expressions idiomatiques à un vocabulaire français (ou parfois anglais *francisé*). Bref, on appela ce langage « franglais » ou « frenglish ». Pour une raison ou pour une autre, cet état de choses fut longtemps accepté par la profession, sans doute parce que le public qui entendait ce langage, connaissant les deux langues, n'en était pas choqué, ni perplexe, puisqu'il comprenait aisément le message exprimé... Quelqu'un ne connaissant qu'une seule des deux langues aurait-il toujours compris le message ?

Depuis quelques années cependant, peut-être sous l'influence du principe de *diversité,* qui tend à promouvoir le respect des autres cultures, le désir de ne pas déformer leur langue semble être apparu. Quelle qu'en soit la raison, la grammaire est peu à peu revenue dans les classes, avec toutes ses différences entre l'anglais et le français. Or ces différences sont souvent, pour chacune des deux langues, l'expression d'une façon particulière de penser, l'expression d'une certaine logique.

Comparons quelques exemples qui illustreront ces différences de logique ou de vision entre l'anglais et le français :

1) Lorsqu'un Américain « ***gets on*** the bus », le Français « ***monte dans*** le bus ». Une même situation, deux façons de la concevoir : tandis que le français exprime ici une verticalité (*monter = to climb up*) et un espace, un volume (*dans*), l'anglais voit la situation comme un mouvement de l'extérieur vers l'intérieur (*to get in = to enter*) et le bus comme une surface (*on*). L'anglais *to get, to enter* n'exprime pas du tout la verticalité. Or les deux façons de voir sont valables; une réalité a toujours de multiples facettes et chaque langue choisit et présente la sienne, excluant les autres facettes.

2) Un buveur de bière américain commandera « ***a draft beer*** », c'est-à-dire une bière tirée (*drawn out, pulled out*) d'un baril (*a keg*). Le buveur français demandera « ***une bière à la pression*** », c'est-à-dire poussée (*pushed out from within*) par la pression carbonique du baril.

3) Un Américain « walks ***in*** the rain, and comes ***out*** of the rain ».

Un Français « marche ***sous*** la pluie » et « ne reste pas ***sous*** la pluie ».

La langue anglaise représente la pluie comme image visuelle et en terme d'intériorité/extériorité (*in, out*); la langue française la présente par déduction : puisque la pluie vient d'en haut (*from above*), on est donc dessous (*underneath*).

4) Lorsqu'un Américain dit : « ***I'll trade my watch for yours*** », par contraste, un Français dira : « J'échange ma montre ***contre*** la tienne ». La langue anglaise souligne l'idée de but, d'intention, et le français en termes d'opposition : le mouvement des deux objets (les montres) se fait dans chaque direction opposée. Et pourtant (*yet*) la situation est identique.

Il suffit par exemple d'explorer les diverses catégories grammaticales (p. ex. les articles, les temps de verbes, le subjonctif, la place de l'adjectif, etc.) selon la logique de leur propre système pour en découvrir l'aspect culturel. On entend parfois dire en effet : « *Language is culture* », alors que la culture est recherchée le plus souvent dans d'autres domaines (p. ex. littérature, beaux-arts, musique, coutumes, traditions, symboles, etc.).

Or ce livre, à la différence des grammaires traditionnelles, tente d'explorer la culture telle qu'elle se manifeste, parfois subtilement, **_dans_** et **_par_** le langage même. Les analyses qui y sont présentées sont à la portée d'étudiants de deuxième ou de troisième années de français. Une approche raisonnée devrait ainsi inspirer le désir de s'exprimer et de communiquer dans un français *authentique*.

Soulignons que ce livre est *un complément* pour n'importe quelle méthode d'apprentissage de la langue. Son but est de promouvoir l'ambition et les moyens de maintenir, tel un train sur les rails, le droit chemin qui mène à *la langue telle qu'on la pense*.

Jacques Bourgeacq

Objective and Structure of the Book

The title of this book, *Le français tel qu'on le pense*, echoes another familiar and frequent title, *Le français tel qu'on le parle*, which a number of authors used throughout the 20th century with various topics and objectives, mostly to emphasize the different levels of language (standard, literary, colloquial, slang, etc.), or the different types of French over time and in various regions. [2]

This approach is not strictly grammatical, but *stylistic*, insofar as it seeks, in expressing a given idea, a plurality of options, stressing the search for nuances. The plurality of options is precisely what defines the term *stylistics*. The goal is to provide inquisitive students of French explanations for **standard** French usage which, in the course of their study, they often find either confusing, odd or unnatural. Whenever possible, discussions will extend beyond the purely descriptive to the "logical" or historical principles underlying each specific language pattern or micro-system at hand. Practical advice will often accompany theoretical explanations.

As the subtitle indicates (i.e. *Elements of...*), this book does not offer a comprehensive study of French usage, and it focuses primarily on those areas where our teaching experience has been shown to present stumbling blocks and confusion for English speakers.

Occasionally, discussions will center on points in the history of language. Those discussions are designed to stress the nature of language as an ever-changing, dynamic organism. They add a much needed historical and cultural dimension to the depth of language study.

---
2   Among others, Françoise Gadet, a sociolinguist on the linguistic variations over different eras and regions; Renée White, on current idioms, slang, sayings and proverbs.

Jacques Bourgeacq

To the student

Each chapter includes a set of practical exercises designed to further internalize the principles and explanations presented, and to reinforce retention of the contents.

Exercises aim at helping you deepen and refine your active knowledge of French, both rational and affective, and **within the limitations of the language itself.** The objective is not to turn you into a walking French grammar manual, but rather to enable you to allow the structures and patterns of French to sink in, eventually reaching the point of instinctive **sensing,** expressing your idea in **what is real** French, and understanding **what simply cannot be**. These exercises focus on real texts, to better explore the various options afforded by a specific context.

A glossary of grammatical terms is included at the end of the book to help students familiarize themselves with, or refresh their memory on basic grammar concepts. At the beginning of each chapter, some general grammatical concepts and terms are also included.

Jacques Bourgeacq

Chapter 1

The articles

Les articles

The Basic System

We may begin by asking what the purpose of ***articles*** is. Some languages have no articles, or few articles; others have an elaborate system of articles. French and English both have complex systems. Articles basically present nouns in a certain light (as an abstract idea, a concrete reality, totally or partially, as something specific, as a single element or as a group, etc.), all in relation to a stated situation on hand. This highlights the importance of context in selecting appropriate articles. This chapter attempts to find some order and logic in the French viewpoint regarding the world of nouns <u>**as presented**</u> by these little but essential particles called articles. Another way to say "as presented" is ***actualizing***, namely bringing a virtual concept (i.e. a noun found in the dictionary) into the ***actual*** life of a text. French and English do not always coincide indeed in their ***actualizing*** of nouns.

We often hear that French, as well as the other Romance languages (Spanish, Italian, Portuguese, Romanian, Catalan, etc.) *come from* Latin. In reality, it would be more exact to say that, to a great extent, these languages <u>are</u> Latin, but *spoken* Latin, that has evolved differently in contact with the various local cultures and languages that were already spoken throughout the Roman Empire. This accounts for both the similarities and differences found among these Romance languages.

Meanwhile, written Latin remained intact throughout the centuries, set in manuscript or scroll form, and became the so-called "dead language" that we hear about today. From this perspective, and in some way, *spoken* Latin is still alive, though it has greatly evolved.

Now, there were no such things as articles in Latin. Speakers of Latin, however, must have used frequently their existing *demonstrative* adjectives to present nouns verbally with greater expressivity. These demonstratives were carried over into the various regions of the empire.

In the case of French, the definite articles *le, l', la, les* derive from a class of Latin demonstrative adjectives: il**le**, il**la**, il**los**, il**las** (= *this, that, these,* etc.). This explains why articles, like demonstratives, often act as fingers pointing to the things, persons or ideas they designate. This <u>*deictic*</u> feature (i.e. finger pointing) is present in both English and French:

I knew **the** *man (= this man) was lying.*

Je savais que **l'***homme (= cet homme) mentait.*

As in English, the definite article is most often used to <u>particularize</u> the noun it modifies:

Rendez-moi **la** *vidéo* ***que je vous ai prêtée.*** (a particular video)

C'est **le** *professeur* ***dont je vous parlais.*** (a particular person)

Unlike English, however, a noun viewed as a general notion, as an abstraction, will take a definite article:

I like wine. (no article)   *J'aime* **le** *vin.*

I don't like wine. (no article)   *Je n'aime pas* **le** *vin.*

In the above case, we do not refer to a specific wine, but as the expression goes, we have in mind "the very idea of it," namely "wine" as a definite abstract concept. And whether you like wine or not, it remains just a concept <u>in this specific context</u>. For the same reason, abstract notions from a French perspective, such as *l'amour,* **la** *joie,* **la** *charité,* **les** *vacances,* take a definite article.

An added reason may be that such abstractions are so familiar in the culture, that they clearly refer to themselves: ie. <u>that</u> *particular, well-known feeling called joy* = **la** *joie,* **la** *sensation* **appelée joie**. And even concrete things (vin, bière, jambon), whenever viewed as a general idea, will take the definite article, like any abstract idea:

L'amour est aveugle.   Love is blind. (no article in English)

Aimez-vous **la** *bière ? Do you like beer?* (no article in English)

Now compare:

--*Voulez-vous* **de la** *bière ou* **du** *vin ?* (partitive article)

--*D'habitude, je préfère* **le** *vin, mais comme j'ai très soif*

  aujourd'hui, je prendrai **de la** *bière; mais* **une** *bière légère.*

In this brief dialogue, we have used three different articles, depending on our immediate presentation of each of these beverages <u>throughout the various steps of this particular context</u>: the partitive article (*du, de la, des*) to express an unspecified quantity, the definite article (*le, l', la les*) to express a general idea, and the indefinite article (*un, une, des*) to express one usual quantity or serving.

Note that the verb *préférer* suggests an abstract idea, while *prendre* naturally points to a concrete thing. Nothing, however, keeps us from viewing *préférer* as a concrete choice, given the appropriate context:

Aujourd'hui, je préfère **de la** *bière. Je préfère* **une** *bière.* (**préférer** means here **prefer to drink**).

Now, what happens to the partitive or indefinite articles in a negative sentence? We are dealing here with concrete realities:

*I don't want wine. Je ne veux pas **de** vin.* (no article)

*I don't have glasses. Je n'ai pas **de** verres.* (no article)

In a negative sentence, whether partitive or indefinite, the article disappears (by French logic: no wine, no glasses to point to), leaving only the preposition **de**, which, as we have seen earlier, was part of both articles in an affirmative sentence. The partitive, as its name indicates, means *part **of the*** (= **de + le, la or les**) total existing quantity (like *some* or *any* in English).

Note: We may say, however: "J'ai commandé de la bière, pas du vin," in a situation in which wine was served by error.

What transpires from all these examples is *the importance of the context* in evaluating our view of the situation and selecting each appropriate article. And as English has its own viewpoint and logic, so does French. It is easier to accept such differences if we understand their logic.

In the plural:

Switching now to the indefinite article, it is clear that *un/une* stemmed from the Latin numeral (*unus, una*). The indefinite article in the plural (**des**) derives, as was said above, from the partitive article (a contraction of **de + les**). However, it is not to be confused with the partitive article, which is a *singular* form, whereas the plural indefinite article (**des**) modifies things or persons that can be counted:

*I have **a** friend. J'ai **un** ami.*

I have friends. (no article in English) *J'ai **des** amis.*

*I don't have friends. Je n'ai pas **d'**amis.* (no friend, therefore no **des**, since it would mean *de +les*).

Now the partitive plural **des** occurs when a countable item is viewed as a whole group:

Countable:

*I steal **a** French fry. Je te vole **une** frite.* (indefinite)

*I steal (some) French fries. Je te vole **des** frites.* (indefinite)

Non-countable:

*I ordered French fries. J'ai commandé **des** frites.*

*I did not order French fries. **Je n'ai pas** commandé **de** frites.*

(partitive, as we view *fries* here as a bulk, a serving that is not sensed as countable; note also *de* for zero fries, in the negative sentence).

There are just a few plural nouns that are ***essentially*** partitive, namely having no singular form, when presented as a quantity:

*I ate spinach. J'ai mangé **des** épinards.* (as we cannot count one spinach, two spinaches, etc.!).

The same for *pasta (**des** pâtes), maths (**des** mathématiques), people (**des** gens), vacation (**des** vacances)*, etc.

Note: For some unclear reason, the above nouns are always in the plural.

There is an area where the article can be problematic: the case when a noun modifies another noun. This situation is extremely frequent. An example of this is a ***garage door***.

Now in this case, two situations will occur, showing the importance of the context:

1) If we say: *I have to buy **a garage door***, the noun ***garage*** functions here as an adjective, since it adds a characteristic to the noun ***door***, indicating the type of door.

<u>In French</u>: *Je dois acheter* **une** *porte de garage*. (no article, as *garage* has lost its status as a noun to function as an adjective).

2) If we say: *Please go and close* **the garage door**, the word **garage** retains its status as a noun, since what is understood here is <u>not</u> a type of door, but rather an existing door.

<u>In French</u>: *Veux-tu aller fermer* **la** *porte* **du** *garage. (a definite article (***du** = **de** + **le***), since we are dealing here with a specific garage with a specific door!)*

This last topic will be discussed in greater details in the chapter about the <u>complements of nouns</u> (Chapter 3). At this time, let us point out that a noun is often called a *substantive*, as it stands for a <u>substance</u>, contrasting with an adjective, which adds only a characteristic to a noun.

<u>Other typical cases:</u>

1. Unlike English, French articles tend to be repeated in a series of nouns:

Nous avons **des** *dollars,* **des** *euros et* **des** *francs suisses.*

2. <u>With nationalities, religions, professions</u>, the article tends to be omitted when it is sensed as an adjective:

He is **a** *doctor.* **Il** *est médecin.* (a characteristic: no article)

But: *He is* **an** *excellent doctor.* **C'**est **un** *médecin excellent.* (When characterized by an adjective, the noun regains its full status as a noun. The case of <u>*c'est*</u> vs. <u>*il est*</u> is discussed in Chapter 4).

3. <u>In some phrases where the noun preceded by a preposition functions as an</u> ***adverb*** (i.e. describing a circumstance of the action), the article is omitted, as in English:

She works **with courage**. *Elle travaille* **avec courage**. (replaces the adverb *courageusement*)

But: *Elle travaille avec **un** courage **admirable**.* (the adjective *admirable* gives back to *courage* its full status as a noun, so the article returns).

This absence of an article also occurs in many adverbial phrases, probably handed down from Old French, such as:

*une distance **à vol d'oiseau*** (a distance as the crow flies)

*rencontrer **à mi-chemin*** (meet halfway)

*parler **à coeur ouvert*** (speak from the heart)

*témoigner **de vive voix*** (testify face to face, in person)

*décider **en fin de compte*** (decide ultimately, at the end of the day)

4. The definite article will replace a possessive adjective with parts of the body, the possessive connection being obvious:

*Raise **your** hand. Levez **la** main.*

*Sa mère **lui** lave **les** mains.* (lui = à son enfant)

*Je **me** lave **les** mains.*

All these situations particularize the nouns as a matter of self-evidence; English prefers to use possessive adjectives. French emphasizes the whole person rather than parts of the body.

Note: Similar cases occur in English. Compare:

*I kicked **his** leg.*

*I kicked **him** in **the** leg.* (Is there a difference in how the situation is presented?)

On the other hand, English seems to make no linguistic distinction between *I wash **my** clothes* and *I wash **my** hands.* --> *Je lave **mon** linge / Je **me** lave **les** mains.*

5. <u>Proper names</u> are considered self-determinant, and thus need <u>no</u> article:

Dieu, Shakespeare, Einstein.

But: ***Le Dieu d'Abraham*** (Abraham seems to particularize Dieu, emphasizing <u>one specific facet</u> of the concept of God).

6. <u>Articles are usually omitted before a text title</u>:

A History of the United States

Histoire des Etats-Unis

The assassination of President Kennedy

***Assassinat du** Président Kennedy* (in a newspaper or as a book title)

7. <u>Addressing someone directly vs. referring to someone</u>:

*Bonjour **Professeur** Duval.* (no article in addressing; note the capital letter for **P**rofesseur, since it is a title).

*J'ai rendez-vous aujourd'hui avec **le** professeur Duval.* (in contrast with English, a reference to a person's status or profession requires an article. Note also that *professeur* is not capitalized, as it is used here as a common noun).

8. <u>In a list of things or persons</u>, the article can sometimes be omitted for a stylistic effect of compactness or acceleration:

***Des** voitures, **des** autobus et **des** vélos circulaient dans la rue.*

***Voitures, autobus et vélos** circulaient dans la rue.*

9. <u>In most cases, names of countries</u> are preceded by a definite article: *La France, l'Espagne et l'Italie sont en Europe.*

Note: The preposition *en* with the name of a country or region takes no article. In fact, *en* very rarely takes an article in any given situation, probably because it forms <u>an adverbial phrase</u> (a situation) with a noun, which thus loses its substantive force: e.g. *en **vacances**, en avion, en guerre.* There are a few exceptions, however, handed down from the Middle Ages: *en l'air, en l'an 1910, en l'absence de, en l'occurrence,* etc.

Some islands take no article: à *Cuba,* à *Madagascar,* à *Maurice,* à *Tahiti,* à *Hawaii,* à *Puerto Rico,* etc.

But: à **la** *Martinique,* à **la** *Guadeloupe,* à **la** *Réunion.*

Note: *En Martinique* and *en Guadeloupe* are used more often today.

10. <u>Most grammar books state that with adjectives of quantity</u> (coined from *adverbs +de*) such as **beaucoup <u>de</u>, peu <u>de</u>, trop <u>de</u>,** etc. the article is omitted, providing no explanation why:

Examples:

*Nous avons **des** amis.*

*Nous avons **beaucoup** d'amis.*

*Il me reste **beaucoup de** vin dans ma cave.*

<u>A possible explanation for this omission</u>: As the preposition *de* is an integral part of both the partitive and indefinite articles, we would normally expect the phrase **beaucoup de** (= *much* or *many of*) to be followed by the articles **du, de la, des.** Apparently, this potential <u>alliteration</u> (**de des, de du, de de la*) has been avoided by <u>dropping the article altogether</u>.

But, logically, the article comes back when the situation requires a <u>definite</u> article instead of partitive or indefinite:

Compare:

*Il me reste **du** vin.*

*Il me reste beaucoup **de** vin.* (partitive ***du*** is dropped))

*Il me reste beaucoup **du** vin **que vous m'avez vendu.***

(now ***vin*** is no longer viewed as a mere quantity, but as a <u>specific, definite</u> item: the one that was sold; so <u>beaucoup **de**</u> blends with ***le***, contracting into ***du***, thus *beaucoup du*).

11. As in case number 10 above, <u>a number of French verbs take the preposition **de**</u> to connect with a noun object: *avoir besoin **de**, avoir envie **de**, se servir **de***, etc.

Let us observe what happens with two verbs, one taking a direct object, ***Vouloir***, and another taking an indirect object with ***de***, ***Avoir besoin de***. The situation is identical for both, requiring normally a partitive article:

I want some coffee.

*Je veux **du** café.*

I need some coffee.

*J'ai besoin **de** café.* (no article: avoiding ****de du***).

As a general rule, it can be said that the preposition ***de*** and the partitive article (***du, de la de l', des***) are "allergic" to each other. And the verb's preposition ***de*** always wins! To avoid a clash (****de du, de de la, de des***, etc.), the partitive article drops out of the picture. It can truly be said that, despite its logic, ***de*** is <u>*the*</u> "nuisance" French preposition!

12. <u>Let us continue to observe other situations that occur when a vast number of verb phrases using the preposition **de** encounter a partitive or indefinite article.</u>

Compare:

*Mon jardin est entouré **d'une** clôture.*

*Mon jardin est entouré **de la** clôture **que mon père a installée**.*

*Mon jardin est entouré **d'a**rbres.* (the article *des* has dropped out)

*Mon jardin est entouré **des** arbres **que mon père a plantés**.* (here, *des* = *de* + *les*, since *arbres* is stated as specific).

*un château entouré **d'un** fossé*   A castle surrounded by **a** ditch

*un château entouré **de** fossés* (here *des* has dropped out to avoid a clash with the preposition *de*)   A castle surrounded by ditches

Note: Again, in the plural, the indefinite article *des* is omitted to avoid the alliteration **de des*. If I switch from *de* to *par*, the article *des* then reappears: *un château entouré **par des** fossés...* The same would be the case with all the examples listed above.

13. <u>In many verbal expressions which form a close-knit unit</u>, the article was dropped. This process probably began in the Middle Ages, when nouns often had no articles yet and acquired them gradually later. The following familiar expressions thus go back far into time: ***avoir faim, avoir soif, avoir froid, avoir affaire à, avoir envie***, etc.

Compare:

J'ai faim.

But: *J'ai **une** faim de loup.* (I'm so hungry, I could eat a horse)

Just a few other cases:

I **put an end** to the situation.	*J'ai **mis fin** à la situation.*
Let's **take this into account**.	*Tenons **compte** de cela.*
This medal **brings** me **luck**.	*Cette médaille me **porte chance**.*

We closed **_the_ shop**.	Nous avons **fermé boutique**.

All these considerations may seem overwhelming at first reading. The main rule to retain is *Always keep sight of the immediate viewpoint of each noun* (abstract? general? specific? partitive? etc.), as it appears in turn into the context (the situation) at hand. Practice will do the rest. What will have been gained is a deeper, more rational sense of the French logic pertaining to the use of articles.

EXERCISES

1. Explain the use of articles (including the absence of article before a noun) in the following text.

This is an excerpt from Légendes rustiques, by novelist George Sand from the oral tradition of her region of origin in France. The "lupeux" is a version of the "loup-garou," a werewolf of ancient superstition:

Le lupeux est un démon dont la nature n'a jamais été bien définie et dont l'apparaissance varie suivant les localités. C'est encore au pays de Brenne qu'il fait sa résidence, dans ces interminables plaines semées d'étangs immenses qui ont tous leur légende et où vivent les grands serpents donneurs de fièvres, cousins germains des cocadrilles que l'on aperçoit quand les eaux sont basses, mais que l'on ne peut détruire qu'en desséchant les marécages où ils résident depuis que le monde est monde.

Un de nos amis, qui parcourait le pays avec un guide, entendit, un soir dans le crépuscule, une voix presque humaine et très douce, qui, d'un ton enjoué ou plutôt goguenard, répétait de place en place, autour de lui. «Ah! Ah!»

Il regarda de tous côtés, ne vit rien et dit à son compagnon de route: «Voilà quelqu'un de bien étonné; est-ce à cause de nous?» (George Sand, Légendes rustiques, A. Morel et Cie, Paris, 1858)

2. **Complete the following text with appropriate articles, and identify the cases in which no article should be used. Explain those cases.**

This text is an excerpt from short story writer Alphonse Daudet's Lettres de mon moulin. *A summer walk in Provence...*

C'était en revenant de Nîmes, _____ après-midi de juillet. Il faisait _____ chaleur accablante. A perte de vue(**1**), _____ route blanche, embrasée, poudroyait entre _____ jardins de _____ oliviers et de _____ petits chênes, sous _____ grand soleil de _____ argent mat qui remplissait tout _____ ciel. Pas _____ tache de _____ ombre, pas _____ souffle de _____ vent. Rien que _____ vibration de _____ air chaud et _____ cri strident de _____ cigales, musique folle, assourdissante, à temps pressés, qui semble _____ sonorité même de cette immense vibration lumineuse... Je marchais en plein désert(**2**) depuis deux heures, quand tout à coup(**3**), devant moi, _____ groupe de _____ maisons blanches se dégagea de _____ poussière de _____ route. (A. Daudet, Lettres de mon moulin, Hetzel, 1869)

3. **Same exercise as the preceding one. Whenever two solutions are possible, name and explain them.**

This text is an excerpt from 19th century author Eugène Fromentin's semi-autobiographic novel, Dominique. *The narrator recalls his youth as an orphan adopted by the owner of a provincial house, in which he enters for the first time...*

J'entrai dans _____ maison de _____ Maître Ceyssac, comme on franchit _____ seuil de _____ prison.

C'était _____ vaste maison, située dans _____ quartier, non pas _____ plus désert, mais _____ plus sérieux de _____ ville, confinant à _____ couvents, avec _____ très petit jardin qui moisissait dans _____ ombre de _____ hautes clôtures, _____ grandes chambres sans _____ air et sans _____ vue, _____ vestibules sonores, _____ escalier de _____ pierre tournant dans _____ cage obscure et trop peu de _____ gens pour animer tout cela.

On y sentait _____ froideur de _____ mœurs anciennes et _____ rigidité de _____ mœurs de _____ province, _____ respect de _____ habitudes, _____ loi de _____ étiquette, _____ aisance, _____ grand bien-être et _____ ennui.

(E. Fromentin, <u>Dominique</u>, Revue des deux mondes, 1862)

4. **Same exercise as the preceding one.**

This next text is an excerpt from Guinean writer Camara Laye's autobiographical novel, <u>L'enfant noir</u>. The description of an African private hut... (Several options in the use of articles may indicate the intended audience for the text: Guinean readers or Western readers?)

Mon père avait là sa case à proximité de _____ atelier, et souvent je jouais là, sous _____ véranda qui l'entourait. C'était _____ case personnelle de mon père. Elle était faite de _____ briques en _____ terre battue et pétrie avec _____ eau; et comme toutes nos cases, ronde et fièrement coiffée de _____ chaume. On y pénétrait par _____ porte rectangulaire. A l'intérieur, _____ jour avare tombait de _____ petite fenêtre. A droite, il y avait _____ lit, en _____ terre battue comme _____ briques, garni de _____ simple natte en _____ osier tressé et de _____ oreiller bourré de _____ kapok. (Camara Laye, <u>L'enfant noir</u>, copyright© Plon, 1953)

Chapter 2

The qualifying adjective

L'adjectif qualificatif

What is an adjective? As we shall see later, there are several types of adjectives: descriptive, possessive, demonstrative, interrogative, etc. In this chapter, we concern ourselves only with the qualifying (or descriptive) adjective.

As a general term, the word ***adjective*** stems from the Latin preposition ***ad*** + the verb ***jacere***, meaning *"throw towards."* A qualifying adjective is thus a word "thrown toward" a noun, to <u>add</u> to it a certain detail (form, size, color, quality, property, age, etc.).

In the case of the qualifying adjective, the noun is made more precise by this added detail, while at the same time it is reduced in meaning, since that detail temporarily excludes from the mind other potential characteristics of this noun.

<u>Example:</u>

*I own a **white** horse. Je possède un cheval **blanc**.*

The added characteristic makes the image of the horse more visually precise, while at the same time excluding horses of different colors (no pun intended!). This linguistic process reminds us of a photographic zoom lens, whereby the lens clarifies and amplifies the focused object, while fading or pushing aside its surroundings.

As we well know, one basic difference between English and French is that the French adjective will vary in form, depending on the gender and number of the noun it is attached to:

Un cheval **blanc** *Des chevaux* **blancs**

Une vache **blanche** *Des vaches* **blanches**

Another important difference between the two languages is the **place** that an adjective can take in relation to the noun, before or after the noun. In the Middle Ages, French adjectives were often placed before the noun. Over the centuries, the place became more fluid, as many adjectives gradually migrated to the other side. A number of them remained before the noun, usually those that were very short and particularly vague and subjective in descriptive value: *beau, petit, grand, bon*, etc., which are of a relative and subjective nature. These adjectives describe more the eyes of the beholder than the object beheld.

In traditional textbooks of French, this question of the place of adjectives is treated most often in a purely grammatical and mechanical framework, and thus receives very little **semantic** attention (i.e. attention to their meaning). Yet the adjective belongs also in the vocabulary domain since, as we shall see, **it is the meaning of the adjective that often determines its place**. Its grammatical dimension (it has one since the place of words pertains to syntax) is often a result of its semantic meaning.

Traditional textbooks frequently present this question by saying that, unlike English, French adjectives are usually placed after the noun, which is only partly true. These grammars then proceed to list a series of exceptions, including those, now illustrious, "*adjectives that change meaning according to their place.*" While true, it seems this explanation is putting the cart before the horses, namely confusing the cause and the effect. This simplistic explanation, albeit somewhat practical in its mechanical applications, does no justice to the question of *why*, failing to promote a sure *feeling* for this important question. It does not explain those cases that contradict this rule either! So once again, we shall have to explore a certain logic at work in the placing of French adjectives.

Before pursuing our exploration though, it is important to state that, contrary to the popular belief in many French classrooms, ***a great number of French adjectives can be placed either before or after the noun*** (even those describing colors and religions, described as always following the noun).

Examples:

*les maisons **blanches** du Maroc* (distinctive adjective: houses that are white among other houses of different colors in that country)

*les **blanches** maisons du Maroc* (stereotyped adjective: Moroccan houses strike the mind as usually white, whether true or false)

*L'Irlande **catholique***

(that faction, as opposed to the Protestant faction; History precludes placing this adjective before the noun in the situation of Ireland).

*la **catholique** Espagne* (Spain is viewed here as one traditionally

Catholic country, which is plausible).

(Note that such adjectives are not capitalized in French)

We shall also see which category of adjectives **cannot** be placed before the noun and why. The fluidity of the French system of adjectives stems from several factors, separate or combined, which we shall call ***values***.

The Values

1. ***Qualitative value*** (descriptive, distinctive) vs. ***quantitative value*** (numeral) of the adjective:

Example:

*Elle portait ce jour-là une **nouvelle** robe.*

(The dress here is presented in a *chronologica*l order, as part of a series of her previous dresses (third? seventh? 20th, others?). The point of view is <u>quantitative</u> (numeral), not referring at all to the *nature* or *style* of the dress).

*Elle portait ce jour-là une robe **nouvelle**.*

(Now the dress is presented from the viewpoint of a different artistic conception, of a *new style*. The adjective *nouvelle* is therefore <u>descriptive</u>, <u>distinctive</u>, in parallel with the series: *moderne, originale, chic, élégante, dernier cri*, etc.

The above considerations apply also to the list (alluded to earlier) found in traditional textbooks of those "illustrious" adjectives habitually classified as "*changing meaning depending on their place in relation to the noun*," such as *ancien, certain, dernier, différent, divers, même, seul, prochain, propre, unique*, etc. This is again, as the saying goes, putting the cart before the horses, and it does <u>not</u> explain why and how.

Example:

***Différentes** méthodes sont employées.*

The stress here is on the **number** of methods in the series: *une, deux, trois, des, plusieurs, quelques*, etc. The idea of **difference** persists, but it is <u>not</u> what is actually emphasized. To confirm, let us note the absence of an article in the sentence: indeed the adjective ***différentes*** <u>replaces and functions here as the missing article (*des*)</u>.

Now:

*Des méthodes **différentes** sont employées.*

Here the semantic meaning of the adjective is further emphasized by its place: ***différentes*** is <u>distinctive</u>, sensed as fully belonging in the series of: *diverses, distinctes, opposées, identiques, pareilles, semblables, dissemblables,* etc., rather than as a mere numeral.

2. <u>***Affective value***</u> (subjective) vs. <u>***intellectual value***</u> (objective) of the adjective:

Due to the fact that they add a characteristic to the noun, adjectives can capture either the imagination or the intellect. For instance, the adjective ***sordide*** carries, in itself, an ***affective*** (subjective) value. It calls into action our feelings, sense of taste, and imagination. On the other hand, in the expression ***le gaz carbonique*** (carbon dioxide), the adjective ***carbonique*** can only be conceived as having an ***intellectual, technical*** (i.e. objective) value, as it addresses <u>only</u> our rational mind (even if a friend has died from carbon dioxide poisoning, but that's another story!).

Here is another test for determining the place: Something can be ***more or less*** sordid, while carbon dioxide <u>cannot</u> be viewed as ***more or less*** carbon. Adjectives that have an essentially *intellectual value* will <u>always</u> be placed <u>after</u> the noun, as they are <u>totally distinctive</u>. On the other hand, those adjectives that are *affective* (subjective) can be placed on either side of the noun.

Affective adjectives sometimes coincide with <u>***figurative adjectives***</u>.

<u>Examples</u>:

a ***bitter*** fruit (literal meaning) - *un fruit **amer***

a ***bitter*** disappointment (figurative meaning) - *une **amère** déception*

3. <u>**Analytical**</u> value vs. <u>**Synthetic**</u> value of the adjective:

These terms will become clear as we progress into our discussion. When an adjective shows an *intellectual* (objective) value, it is felt as a characteristic <u>added</u> to the noun <u>*as an afterthought*</u>. The noun comes first to our consciousness, and the characteristic that distinguishes it from other parallel characteristics comes later. This is a two-stage process, i.e. an ***analytical*** process.

Example:

In the expression **une affaire sordide**, the adjective (although semantically affective) comes after the noun, because it is felt in this instance as parallel with other possible types of **affaires**: *honnête, légitime, raisonnable, impossible, criminelle*, etc. It is analytical, because at this moment its inherent affective value is less felt and is unstressed.

Now in **une sordide affaire**, we fully emphasize the affective (subjective, emotional) value. It is a primary mental reaction. No comparison with other existing affairs is at play in our mind. The group *adjective + noun* strikes us as **a whole idea**, coming to our mind as a block, in one sole mental operation, affective, subjective. In linguistics, this mental operation is called synthetic, as well as the participating adjective.

Note: Once again, let us emphasize that the speaker is not usually conscious of such mental processes. It is culture that simply expresses itself through the deep structures of the language.

Except for the two extreme classes of adjectives that are either essentially of the *intellectual* category (the **carbonique** type) and those essentially *affective* (the **sordide** type), the vast number of French adjectives can assume both values, depending on the context at hand, and they change place accordingly. It can be claimed that French adjectives enjoy great mobility in relation to nouns.

Our discussion in this chapter suggests not only great mobility and freedom regarding the place of adjectives, but also a wealth of nuances in expressivity. This flexibility results in a greatly enhanced stylistic resource.

In communicating, it is important therefore to be aware of the variable place of the adjectives, if we wish to produce authentic and precise French in our own messages, and to feel the attitude and the viewpoint of other speakers in theirs. That being said, it is true that adjectives tend to follow the noun (but not mandatorily, as implied in many grammar textbooks), since they are often sensed as distinctive.

4. The **past participle** as **adjective**:

Past participles in general can be used as adjectives, as in English.

Examples:

*des bandes **dessinées*** (from the verb *dessiner, to draw*) = **comics**

*une voiture mal **garée*** (from the verb *garer*) = *a car poorly **parked***

So not only will past participles function as adjectives, but also some of them, verbal forms derived from regular adjectives, can bring to a noun a dynamic aspect of transformation.

Examples:

*un papier **jaune*** (static) --> *un papier **jauni** par le temps* (dynamic)

= *a paper **turned yellow*** (from the verb *jaunir*)

*un ciel **obscur*** --> *un ciel **obscurci** par les nuages*

= *obscured, darkened* (from the verb *obscurcir*)

*une salade **fraîche*** --> *une salade **rafraîchie** à l'eau froide*

= *refreshed* (from the verb *rafraîchir*)

*un homme **riche*** --> *un homme **enrichi** par la guerre*

= *made rich* (from the verb *enrichir*)

5. What happens in the case of **multiple adjectives**?

a) if both adjectives have the same value: They are coordinated with **et** or **mais**, and usually follow the noun, as the combination is distinctive.

Examples:

*une étudiante **intelligente et travailleuse*** - *an **intelligent**, **hardworking** student*

*un étudiant **intelligent mais paresseux*** - *an **intelligent but lazy** student*

    b) if one adjective forms a ***synthetic unit*** with the noun: The other adjectives are pushed away from the noun to their usual place.

Examples:

*Une jeune femme **intelligente***

*Une **belle** jeune femme **intelligente***

(*belle* modifies the unit *jeune femme*, and not just *femme*)

*Une jeune femme **belle** et **intelligente***

(*belle* and *intelligente* share here the same parallel value. Here, *belle* becomes distinctive and is pulled to the other side next to *intelligente*).

    6. A special case: **The qualifying adjective vs. the relational adjective.** This case is of special importance to English-speakers, since the English language does not always make a distinction between these two types of adjectives, and thus requires no choice, as does French.

Examples:

*un examen **médical***   (qualifying) --> ***a medical examination***

*un étudiant **en médecine***   (relational) --> ***a medical student***

An examination and a student are indeed not "medical" in the same way. An ***electrical engineer*** is ***un ingénieur électricien*** or ***un ingénieur en électricité***.

Note: It often takes contact with a foreign language to bring to our consciousness certain features of our own native language. This awareness assists in the internalization process.

A final note:

The place of adjectives can also be affected by issues of rhythm. In general, a long adjective will be placed after the noun, especially if the noun is a short word (one or two syllables).

Example:

*J'ai entendu un **cri** épouvantable.*

(one syllable in the noun vs. four in the adjective)

*Un **épouvantable** cri* is indeed a possibility.

It is placed here before the noun for a stylistic effect, to lengthen the scream with this long adjective, in addition to its affective value. We have entered here into the realm of poetry!

EXERCISES

1. Identify and explain the place of the qualifying adjectives in the following text. *This text is an excerpt from Guy de Maupassant's short story "Le Bonheur." The island of Corsica is described:*

Figurez-vous un monde encore en chaos, une tempête de montagnes que séparent des ravins étroits où roulent des torrents; pas une plaine, mais d'immenses vagues de granit et de géantes ondulations de terre couvertes de maquis ou de hautes forêts de châtaigniers et de pins. C'est un sol vierge, inculte, désert, bien que parfois on aperçoive un village, pareil à un tas de rochers au sommet d'un mont. Point de culture, aucune industrie, aucun art. On ne rencontre jamais un morceau de bois travaillé, un bout de pierre sculptée, jamais le souvenir du goût enfantin ou raffiné des ancêtres pour les choses gracieuses et belles. C'est là même ce qui frappe le plus en ce superbe et dur pays : l'indifférence héréditaire pour cette recherche des formes séduisantes qu'on appelle l'art. (G. de Maupassant, "Le bonheur," Le Gaulois, March 16, 1884).

2. **Complete the following text with adjectives in their appropriate form and place. Explain the cases where two solutions are possible.**
This text is also an except from Guy de Maupassant: Cair de lune. It presents a first impression of Mont Saint-Michel.

J'ai visité le Mont Saint-Michel que je ne connaissais pas. Quelle vision quand on arrive comme moi à Avranches, vers la fin du jour. Je poussai un cri d'étonnement : une (démesuré) _____ baie _____ s'étendait devant moi, à perte de vue, entre (écarté/deux) _____ côtes _____ se perdant au loin dans les brumes; et au milieu de cette (jaune/immense) _____ baie _____, sous un ciel d'or et de clarté, s'élevait, (pointu/sombre/étrange) _____ un mont _____ au milieu des sables.

Dès l'aurore, j'allai vers lui. La mer était basse comme la veille au soir et je regardais se dresser devant moi, à mesure que j'approchais d'elle, (surprenant) _____ l'abbaye _____. Après (plusieurs) _____ heures _____ de marche, j'atteignis le (énorme) _____ bloc _____ de pierre qui porte (dominé/petit) _____ la cité _____ par la (grand) _____ église _____. Ayant gravi la (étroit/rapide) _____ rue _____, j'entrai dans (construit/gothique/ la plus admirable) _____ demeure _____ par Dieu sur la terre, vaste comme une ville, pleine de (écrasé/bas) _____ salles _____ sous des voûtes et des (haut) _____ galeries _____ que soutiennent des (frêle) _____ colonnes _____.

(G. de Maupassant, <u>Clair de lune</u>, Editions Monnier, 1883)

3. **Fill in the adjectives in the appropriate form and place. Identify and explain the cases with two possible answers.**

<u>Examples:</u>

-catholique

*La **catholique** Espagne* (synthetic unit made possible by the tradition)

*L'Irlande **catholique*** (analytic and distinctive, as there is also a Protestant Ireland)

-maigre

*un visage **maigre*** (literal meaning: *a thin face*)

*un **maigre** salaire* (figurative meaning; *meager*; but could make you lean, skinny)

Write the version with the adjective to the right of each phrase.

-triste   un métier - _____

                un regard - _____

-simple   une remarque - _____

                une robe - _____

-commun   un compte en banque - _____

                un accord - _____

-pur   du vin - _____

                par méchanceté - _____

-vrai   une histoire - _____

                un idiot - _____

-ancien   l'histoire - _____

                un de mes professeurs - _____

-méchant   pour un dollar - _____

                Attention, chien ! - _____

Jacques Bourgeacq

-seul   un être n'est pas toujours heureux - _____

               « un être vous manque et tout est dépeuplé » (poète Alphonse de Lamartine)- _____

-blanc   la neige des montagnes - _____

               les maisons du Maroc - _____

-noir   une trahison - _____

               l'œil du taureau - _____

-dernier   C'était la semaine de septembre - _____

               Je viens de la voir la semaine - _____

-unique   Cet emploi est une chance (inespérée) - _____

               Il est fils - _____

-même   Il est la bonté - _____

               J'ai fait cette expérience - _____

-nouveau   Christophe Colomb a découvert le monde - _____

               Aldous Huxley a décrit un monde - _____

-riche   Voilà une idée ! - _____

               Quelle générosité pour un homme ! - _____

Côte à Côte 2

-vert   Il portait une cravate pour la Saint-Patrick -
             _____

             Sa mauvaise note lui a valu une réprimande -
             _____

-légitime   Il s'agit d'un cas de défense -
             _____

             C'est mon fils - _____

-fou   une passion - _____

             un homme - _____

-faux   Il a payé avec un billet - _____

             C'est un raisonnement - _____

4. Connect all the elements of each group to form a logical unit. Construct and explain all possible answers.

Examples:

-intelligent, paresseux   *un élève - un élève **intelligent** mais **paresseux*** (negative impression)

*un élève **paresseux** mais **intelligent*** (less unfavorable impression)

-clair, bien présenté   *une thèse - une thèse **claire** et **bien présentée*** (rhythm: longer adjective comes last)

Write the version with the adjective to the right of each phrase.

-petit, confortable   un appartement - _____

-ennuyeux, long   une conférence - _____

49

- pointu, rouge   un toit - _____
- solide, ancien   un bâtiment - _____
- sombre, étroit   une ruelle - _____
- éclairé, seul   la fenêtre - _____
- doux, agréable   un vin - _____
- pas cher, petit, bon   un restaurant - _____
- généreux, jeune, pauvre un homme - _____
- blanc, sec, bon, petit un vin - _____
- épuisant, long   un voyage - _____
- timide, serviable, brave un garçon - _____
- beau, merveilleusement un visage - _____
- ennuyeux, long   un film - _____

Chapter 3

The complement of a noun,

and the complement of an adjective

*Le complément de nom (ou complément déterminatif),
et le complément d'adjectif*

I. The complement of a noun

In English as in French, the qualifying adjective is not the only word that can qualify or characterize a noun. Other words can also achieve the same result.

Examples:

*a landscape **of great beauty***	*un paysage **d'une grande beauté***
*a **breathtaking** landscape*	*un paysage à **couper le souffle***

Most frequently, the English language places the qualifying word or phrase before the modified noun, as it does for an adjective, without a connecting word:

Examples:

*a **garage** door, **a kitchen** chair, a **dining** room, a **race** car*

However, this apparent simplicity in the English syntax may at times affect the clarity of the message. How should we understand the following phrase:

He is a Mexican history teacher?

Is he a Mexican teacher whose discipline is general history? Or is he a teacher (nationality unspecified) *of Mexican history?*

In French:

*C'est un professeur **d'**histoire mexicai**n**.* (masculine gender, Mexican male teacher)

*C'est un professeur **d'**histoire mexicai**ne**.* (feminine gender, Teacher of Mexican history)

Another example found on the Internet:

Famous England football team coach.

Is he the famous coach of a football team of England? Or Is he the coach of a famous football team of England?

In French:

Entraîneur célèbre d'une équipe de football anglaise (famous male coach)

Entraîneur d'une célèbre équipe anglaise de football (male coach of a famous team)

The more complex French system, as we shall see, reduces greatly the risk of ambiguity, as the reader/listener can rely on the text itself, rather than on his/her cultural knowledge (i.e. beyond language) of the situation.

This being said, in French the complement will <u>follow</u> the noun, as any qualifier with a <u>distinctive</u> *value*. In addition, as can be observed, the noun and its complement are connected with a preposition:

*une porte **de garage**, une chaise **de cuisine**, une salle **à manger**, une voiture **de course**, le service **après-vente**,* etc.

Now the question is, which preposition? The choice of the preposition depends on the *semantic* meaning, i.e. the idea that relates the two connected words. The challenge stems from the variety of potential relations:

time *(temps)*, **place** *(lieu)*, **type** *(espèce)*, **total content** *(contenu total)*, **partial content** *(contenu partiel)*, **matter** *(matière)*, **possession**, etc.

Fortunately, the number of prepositions used to connect a complement to its noun is quite small, in most cases: ***à, de, en.***

As a general rule, we use:

1) <u>the preposition ***à*** for</u>:

• <u>a characteristic detail</u>:

*une chemise **à** manches longues*	*a long sleeve shirt*
*la dame **au** chapeau vert*	*the lady with the green hat*
*l'homme **au** masque de fer*	*the man in the iron mask*
*l'homme **à** la barbe blanche*	*the man with the white beard*

• <u>a partial composition</u>:

un moteur à quatre cylindres	*a four-cylinder engine*
une omelette aux champignons	*a mushroom omelette*

- a utilization or destination:

une machine **à** laver	a washing machine
une tasse **à** café	a coffee cup
une cuillère **à** soupe	a soup spoon
un savon **à** mains	a hand soap
un verre **à** vin	a wine glass

- an operating mode:

une machine **à** vapeur	a steam engine
un bateau **à** voile	a sailboat

2) the preposition *de* for:

- time:

le repas **du** soir	the evening meal
un roman **du** XXe siècle	a 20th century novel

- place:

l'appartement **d'**en haut	the upstairs apartment
la porte **de** derrière	the back door
le voisin **d'**à côté	The next door neighbor

- types:

une voiture **de** sport	a sport car
une salle **de** bain	a full bathroom

*une piste **de** course*	*a race track*
*un cabinet **de** médecin*	*a doctor's office*

- a <u>total composition</u>:

*une maison **de** huit pièces*	*an eight room house*
*une salade **de** tomates*	*a tomato salad*

- <u>content</u>:

*une tasse **de** café*	*a cup of coffee*
*un verre **de** vin*	*a glass of wine*

- <u>materials</u>:

*une tasse **de** porcelaine*	*a porcelain cup*
*une pièce **d'**or*	*a gold coin*
*un coeur **d'**or*	*a heart of gold*

(***de*** for metaphoric value, not ***en***)

- a <u>measure</u>:

*un chèque **de** 50 dollars*	*a check **for** 50 dollars*
*une bouteille **d'**un litre*	*a one-liter bottle*

- <u>possession</u>:

<u>le</u> *cabinet **du** médecin*	<u>the</u> *doctor's office*
<u>un</u> *cabinet **de** médecin*	<u>a</u> *doctor's office*

(also a type)

3) The preposition *en* for:

- concrete material:

une montre **en** or	a gold watch
une tasse **en** porcelaine	a porcelain cup

- shape or form:

un toit **en** pointe	a pointed roof
une pièce **en** trois actes	a three-act play

You may have observed the use of various articles in some of the above examples: In the phrase *la dame **au** chapeau vert*, the definite article is used because it means *la dame dont **le** chapeau est vert*. In the phrase *le repas **du** soir*, the definite article is used because it means *le repas qu'on prend **le** soir* (usually in ***the*** evening).

A reminder: Observe the difference between the two phrases below, seen earlier in the book.

*le cabinet **du** médecin* (refers to the office of a particular doctor)

*un cabinet **de** médecin* (refers to a type of office)

Hypothesis:

One case in the use of articles in this type of phrase does not fit in the general logic of the system. For example, in the phrase: *l'homme **au** masque de fer* (*the man in **the** iron mask*), the definite article appears in both English and French, as the mask refers to a famous and ***unique*** object in written history, hence the definite article. If we refer to a gray-bearded man we are seeing in a crowd at this moment, we can indeed refer to him as *l'homme **à** **la** barbe grise,* due to the evidence of that particular object of our glance at this very moment. Otherwise, in general, we would refer to *un homme **à** barbe grise* (without an article = *qui a **une** barbe grise*). So far so good... But in the following situation, we are left with pure speculation:

une crème à **la** vanille	a vanilla cream
une omelette **aux** champignons	a mushroom omelette
du chocolat **au** lait	milk chocolate

The definite *article makes it legitimate to ask: which vanilla? which mushrooms?* And there is no definite answer, unless we think of these ingredients as prestigious at one time in the past (***those*** precious things!) and therefore very definite in our mind... Another hypothesis: *un café au lait* is a café in which ***du*** lait was added (*au* would thus mean *avec du lait*).

There are many such instances of this type, which is why the matter deserved consideration, though unfortunately inconclusive.

II. The complement of an adjective.

Like a noun, an adjective can also receive a complement. It is also connected to the adjective with a preposition.

> **When the complement is a verb** in its infinitive form, the preposition is either ***à*** or ***de***. To determine which of the two prepositions, it may be helpful to recall the meaning of the original Latin prepositions: ***ad*** (that became **à**) meaning ***to, toward, next to***. The original meaning of ***à*** (= *ad*) allows us to suggest an explanation in the following examples.

Examples:

*L'anglais est facile **à** apprendre.*

In this sentence, the preposition ***à*** expresses a movement toward the action of ***apprendre***, as if to say: *...easy if you intend to learn*. Note also that the adjective can be independent from the verb *être*: *Qui connaît une langue facile **à** apprendre ?*

On the other hand, if the adjective is part of an <u>impersonal phrase</u> with *être* (such as **Il est facile**...), the preposition **de** is used. The preposition **de** is either a connecting word void of content, i.e. just a link; or it may reflect one of its Latin meanings: **of** or **concerning** (cf. Lucretius, **De rerum natura**, *Of the Nature of Things*).

<u>Examples</u>:

<u>Il est facile</u> **d'***apprendre l'anglais.*

In this sentence, the pronoun *il* does not refer to the noun *l'anglais*, but to the whole phrase: **apprendre l'anglais**. In fact, we could phrase the sentence in this way: **Apprendre l'anglais** est facile.

French syntax tends to favor the impersonal construction in order to introduce first a basic theme (in this case the idea of ease) before presenting in this very light the situation at hand (which here is *apprendre l'anglais*). This device is designed to arouse the reader's or listener's curiosity.

<u>These are a few useful adjectives with their constructions</u>:

1. With *à*:

<u>Example</u>: *Pierre est* **apte à** *comprendre la situation.*

(<u>a partial list</u>: *bon, premier, dernier, difficile, aisé, malaisé, enclin, habile, lent, prompt, long, prêt, seul, utile*, etc.)

2. With **de**:

<u>Example</u>: *Pierre est* **capable de** *comprendre la situation.*

(<u>a partial list</u>: *incapable, certain, sûr, content, mécontent, ravi, enchanté, curieux, fatigué, fier, furieux, libre, heureux, honteux, impatient, inquiet*, etc.)

3. With **pour** (and adverb **trop** and **assez**):

Examples:

Il est *trop poli pour être* honnête ! (idea of purpose)

Il est *assez intelligent pour* comprendre.

B. **When the complement is a noun**, the preposition is also most often *à* or *de*:

Examples:

Soyez *fidèles à vos principes.*

J'étais *âgé de 25 ans.*

However, and depending on which adjective, other prepositions can also be used: ***avec, en, pour, envers, après***. In this case, usage is rather capricious, dictated by each individual adjective! There is no known rationale for it.

Examples:

Soyez ***bons pour*** les animaux.

Il est ***fâché avec*** son frère.

Je suis ***reconnaissant envers*** ma mère.

Elle est ***forte en*** mathématiques.

EXERCISES

1. Identify the complements of nouns and complements of adjectives. Explain also the use or absence of articles with these complements.

This text is an excerpt of Alphonse Daudet's Lettres de mon moulin. *An old musician tells the story of the decline of windmills in Provence...*

Imaginez-vous pour un moment, chers lecteurs, que vous êtes assis devant un pot de vin tout parfumé, et que c'est un vieux joueur de fifre qui vous parle.

Notre pays, mon bon monsieur, n'a pas toujours été un endroit mort et sans renom, comme il est aujourd'hui. Autre temps, il s'y faisait un grand commerce de meunerie, et, à dix lieues à la ronde, les gens des *mas* nous apportaient leur blé à moudre... Tout autour du village, les collines étaient couvertes de moulins à vent. De droite et de gauche, on ne voyait que des ailes qui viraient au mistral par-dessus les pins, des ribambelles de petits ânes chargés de sacs montant et dévalant le long des chemins; et toute la semaine c'était plaisir d'entendre sur la hauteur le bruit des fouets, le craquement de la toile et le *Dia hue !* des aides-meuniers... Le dimanche nous allions aux moulins, par bandes. Là-haut, les meunières étaient belles comme des reines, avec leur fichus de dentelles et leurs croix d'or. (A. Daudet, Lettres de mon moulin, Hetzel, 1869)

2. Complete the following text by filling in the adjectives and complements of nouns in the proper form and place.

This text is an excerpt of François-René de Chateaubriand's Le génie du christianisme. The author theorizes on architecture as an imitation of nature.

Les forêts ont été les temples (Divinité, premier), et les hommes ont pris dans les forêts l'idée (architecture, premier). Cet art a donc dû varier selon les climats. Les Grecs ont tourné la colonne (élégant, corinthien) avec son chapiteau (feuilles) sur le modèle (palmier). Les piliers (énorme) du style (vieux égyptien) représentent le sycomore, le figuier (oriental), et la plupart des arbres (Asie, Afrique, gigantesque).

Les forêts (Gaules) ont passé à leur tour dans les temples de nos pères, et nos bois (chênes) ont ainsi maintenu leur origine (sacré). Ces voûtes (en feuillages, ciselé), ces jambages qui appuient les murs et finissent brusquement comme des troncs (brisé), la fraîcheur (voûtes), les ténèbres (sanctuaire), les ailes (obscur), les passages (secret), les portes (abaissé), tout retrace les labyrinthes (bois) dans l'église (gothique); tout en fait sentir l'horreur (religieux), les mystères et la divinité. Les tours (hautain, deux, planté) à l'entrée de l'édifice, surmontent les ormes et les ifs (cimetière), et font un effet (pittoresque) sur l'azur (ciel). (F.-R. de Chateaubriand, <u>Le Génie du christianisme</u>, Granier Frères, 1828)

3. **Combine adjectives and complements of nouns in the phrases below, and explain your constructions.**

<u>Examples</u>:

(vert, chapeau)   la dame

*la dame **au** chapeau vert*   (*au* used for a characteristic detail)

(beau, ravir)   une fillette

*une fillette belle **à** ravir*   (*à* + *infinitive* for intensity; *belle* drawn to the other side by its complement)

Write your answers in the spaces to the right.

-long, 300 pieds   un navire- _____

-huit pièces, vendre   une maison- _____

-trois chambres, louer   un appartement- _____

-son père, digne   C'est <u>le</u> fils...- _____

-son père, digne   C'est <u>un</u> fils...- _____

-soulagement, grand   un soupir- _____

-faire, difficile   un exercice- _____

-montagnes, bien chaud, fort   un café- _____

-pur, joli, or   un bracelet- _____

-massif, chêne, grand   un buffet- _____

-de mathématiques, bon   une élève- _____

-en mathématiques, bon   une élève- _____

-mon père, ancien   un ami- _____

-100 pieds, haut   un bâtiment- _____

-1000 pieds, haut   un bâtiment- _____

-rire, fort   une envie- _____

4. Translate the following phrases, and explain your choices.

<u>Examples</u>:

un verre à vin (utilization, destination)   *a wine glass*

un verre à pied (characteristic detail)   *a stem glass*

Write your translations in the spaces to the right.

a tea spoon _____

a coffee cup _____

an African journey _____

a chocolate cake _____

a check for 50 dollars _____

a medical student _____

a mechanical engineer _____

a flying saucer _____

a fishing village _____

Côte à Côte 2

her married name _____

her married daughter _____

the French consul _____

the girl next door _____

in late October _____

in early June _____

the bridge on the River Kwai _____

the door on the right _____

Take the first door on the right _____

a gasoline engine _____

a periodical exam _____

the periodical room (in a library) _____

congressional elections _____

Jacques Bourgeacq

Chapter 4

The pronoun system: Some problematic cases

Le système des pronoms : quelques cas problématiques

A ***pronoun*** is a word that <u>replaces</u> a noun (Latin ***pro*** = *for, on behalf of*). As seen in the preceding chapter, a pronoun must not be confused with an adjective (***ad + jacere*** = *added to*).

<u>Examples</u>:

Quel *chanteur préférez-vous ?* (adjective)

Lequel *des deux chanteurs préférez-vous ?* (pronoun)

This chapter does not undertake a comprehensive study of all pronouns, as it is assumed they have been introduced at the elementary level of French studies. In this and the next chapter, we have instead a different set of objectives:

1) to facilitate a rational grasp of the various systems.

2) to focus on certain persistent stumbling blocks that English speakers encounter in their use of French pronouns.

I. The Interrogative pronouns:

Grammar manuals often give the impression that there are many interrogative pronouns: *qui ? que ? qu'est-ce qui ? qu'est-ce que ? à quoi ? à quoi est-ce que ? qu'est-ce que c'est que ? lequel (auquel, duquel), lequel est-ce que ?*, etc.

Actually, there are only <u>four</u> interrogative pronouns: *qui, que, quoi, lequel* (and its forms). The words and phrases that are attached to the pronouns are constructions to accommodate the syntactic necessities of any given sentence.

Examples:

Que dites-vous ?

Qu'***est-ce que*** vous dites ?

The object pronoun is the same for both (i.e. ***que***). ***Est-ce que*** is simply an emphatic interrogative formula to turn an affirmative sentence into a question. It can be dissected as follows:

Est (verb), ***ce*** = demonstrative pronoun subject of ***est***), the 2nd ***que*** = relative pronoun modifying ***ce*** and object of the verb ***dites***. A literal translation might be: *What* <u>**is it that**</u> *you are saying*?

Another example:

Qui cherchez-vous ? (***qui*** = direct object of verb *cherchez*)

*Qui **est-ce que** vous cherchez ?* (***que*** = object of *cherchez, relates to **ce***)

Qui a découvert l'Amérique ?(***qui*** = subject of verb *a découvert*)

*Qui **est-ce qui** a découvert l'Amérique ?* (2nd ***qui*** = repeated subject of *a découvert, relates to **ce***): It may translate into: *Who **in the world** discovered...*

Note: In all the above sentences the main (the initial) subject or object pronoun ***qui*** remains the same.

In conclusion, these formulas, *est-ce que* and *est-ce qui*, are mere accessories to the **real** interrogative pronouns. Hence the value of learning to diagram a sentence!

There is no need to survey the whole system, as it functions in the same manner. There is one other "issue," however, that needs to be addressed. This is a frequent confusion among English-speakers (and it is an error):

What is the difference... (between X and Y)?

*Qu'est-ce que c'est la différence... (entre X et Y)?

Quelle est la différence entre un avion et un hélicoptère ? (identification, distinction)

One must distinguish between a *definition* and an *identification*:

Qu'est-ce que c'est qu'un avion ? -- C'est une machine qui vole... (definition)

Note: In the sentence with *quelle*, this word is an interrogative adjective, modifying *différence*, not a pronoun.

There is another stumbling block that needs our attention: the situation of the *indirect discourse*, another name for *reported speech* (i.e. speech reported instead of quoted verbatim):

Example:

Il a demandé: « *Qu'est-ce que vous voulez ?* » (direct quote)   He asked: "*What* do you want?" (direct quote)

Il a demandé *ce que* nous voulions. (reported speech)   He asked *what* we wanted. (reported speech)

Let us dissect: Il a demandé *ce*... (and what does *ce* stand for?) Response: It stands for *que nous voulions.* (Another response could have been *cela,* or *ceci,* pointing to an object (or a phrase).

Note: When not modified by an adjectival clause (as above), *ce* accompanies only *être* (*c'est*). With other verbs: *Ceci* me plaît; *cela* m'ennuie.

A final note on *que* and *quoi*:

These two pronouns are actually one and the same. They came from Latin *quem*. The form *quoi* was the result of sentence rhythm: when placed at the <u>final syllable of a syntagm</u> (a unit of meaning), *que* was vocally stressed and was eventually pronounced *quoi*:

Que veux-tu ? (stress on *tu*, which remained unchanged)

A quoi penses-tu ? (two syntagms: stress on *que* --> *quoi*, and stress on unchanged *tu*).

The same phenomenon occurred also with personal pronouns *me* and *moi*, *te* and *toi*, *se* and *soi*:

Ne me regarde pas. (stress on *pas*)

Regarde-moi. (stress on *me* --> *moi*)

Je ne te vois pas souvent, mais je pense à toi. (the rhythmic stress falls on <u>*pas*</u>, <u>*souvent*</u>, <u>*pense*</u>, and then on <u>*toi*</u>).

II. <u>The relative pronouns</u>:

Relative pronouns, of the same Latin origin as the interrogative pronouns, are connecting words. As their name indicates, they <u>relate</u> to nouns and other pronouns by introducing an adjectival clause called <u>relative clause</u> (*une proposition relative*). Like the interrogative pronouns, they are fewer in number than it appears: *qui*, *que*, *quoi*, *dont*, *où*, and *lequel*, (and more rarely *quiconque*). They usually accompany the noun or pronoun they relate to, whether a person or a thing.

Examples:

Voilà l'*employé* **qui** m'a servi. (subject of *a servi*, relates to *l'employé*)

Voilà le *produit* **qui** m'a été utile. (subject of *a été*)

Voilà l'*employé* **que** j'ai consulté. (object of *ai consulté*; relates to *l'employé*)

Voilà le *produit* **que** j'ai acheté. (object of *ai acheté*)

Relative pronouns do not always relate to a stated <u>antecedent</u> (= the word which is related to).

Example:

*I asked **whoever** was willing to listen to me.*   Je me suis adressé à **qui** voulait bien m'écouter.

Je me suis adressé à **quiconque** voulait bien m'écouter. (random person)

Je me suis adressé à **ceux qui** voulaient bien m'écouter. (specific persons)

Note: ***Quiconque*** is from the Latin masculine pronoun *quicumque*, meaning *whoever* or *whomever*.

Another example:

*I often forget **what** (whatever) I was talking about.*

J'oublie parfois de **quoi** je parlais. (unstated antecedent, vague and almost interrogative)

J'oublie parfois **ce dont** je parlais. (antecedent *ce* is slightly more specific, though not as specific as stating the *topic*)

In stark contrast with the English word ***when,*** the French words ***quand*** or ***lorsque*** <u>can never be relative pronouns</u>. Most often, ***où*** is used as an equivalent to the English relative pronoun **when** (not to be confused with the conjunction **when**).

Examples:

*The town **where** I was born...*   *La ville **où** je suis né*

*The day **when** I was born...*   *Le jour **où** je suis né...* (never **quand** or **lorsque**)

With the French word **date**, a form of **lequel** is used:

Example:

*The date **when** the war started is etched in my memory.* - *La date **à laquelle** la guerre commença reste gravée dans ma mémoire.*

The relative pronoun *dont*: The Latin origin of this pronoun is *de unde* (= *from* or *of where*). So **dont** always includes the preposition **de**. This is why one can say: *le pays **dont** je viens*, as well as *le pays **d'où** je viens*.

Dont can replace *de qui, de quoi, duquel, de laquelle, desquels*. etc. It is therefore a catch-all word, very practical and simplifying. But for one exception: after a prepositional phrase containing **de**, such as *à côté de, au-dessus de, en face de*, etc., an appropriate form of **lequel** is needed, probably to avoid duplication of the preposition **de**. Indeed, as we have said earlier, **de** is <u>the</u> "nuisance" or "capricious" preposition: *à côté de* + **dont** would result in too many **de**! (Remember the case of **de** + the partitive article).

Examples:

*Le passager **à côté duquel** j'étais assis...* (never *dont*)

*La maison **en face de laquelle** je me trouvais...* (never *dont*)

Finally, **dont**, meaning **whose**, calls for a syntax that differs from English. A simple example will suffice to show this point:

*The person **whose** son I know...* (***whose*** + object noun + subject + verb)

*La personne **dont** je connais le fils...* (***dont*** + subject + verb + object noun).

III. The demonstrative pronouns

The origin of the demonstrative pronouns is very complex. In its evolution from Latin, before and through the early Middle Ages, the demonstrative pronouns and adjectives underwent many changes. To make a long story short, the pronoun *ce* ended up as a nucleus or "anchor" from which the other demonstrative pronouns were constructed. *Ce* (from Latin *ecce* (= voici), coupled with *isti* and *illi*, two series of Latin demonstratives. The French demonstrative adjectives, in several stages, became *cisti, cist* (*ce cet, cette, ces*) and the pronouns became *cilli, cil* (celui, celle, celles, ceux). The pronoun *ce* (*ecce + hoc*, a third series) became the neutral pronoun which we find in *c'est*.

Ce and all the other pronouns, masculine and feminine, singular and plural, are often coupled with suffixes *ci* and *là*, adverbs of place: *ceci, cela, celui-ci, celui-là,* etc.

Examples:

*Attendre deux mois ! **Cela** ne me convient pas !* (a whole process takes the neuter gender)

*Je préfère **celle-ci** à **celle-là**.* (e.g. between two cars; *voiture* is feminine)

A problematic case:

The distinction between ***c'est*** and ***il est*** has been a source of confusion for generations of English speakers, as both formulas mean *it is,* and sometimes *he is* and *she is.* To tell the two phrases apart, we must view *il est* as an impersonal formula announcing, presenting an idea, while *c'est* recaps what has just been expressed.

Examples:

Il est horrible *de massacrer un peuple !* (this formula stresses the idea of horror, within which the action is categorized)

Massacrer un peuple, c'est horrible *!* (this formula presents the action first, and then comments on it)

However, in a <u>colloquial, spoken style</u>, *c'est* is frequently used instead of *il est*, and it is accepted as correct in casual French:

C'est horrible *de massacrer tout un peuple !*

EXERCISES

1. <u>The interrogative pronouns and adjectives</u>:

A. <u>Fill in the appropriate word in each space, according to the context, and paying attention to the sentence construction</u>.

Examples:

_____ est ta profession ?   --> **Quelle** est ta profession ?

_____ tu veux ?   --> **Qu'est-ce que** tu veux ?

_____ veux-tu ?   --> **Que** veux-tu ?

1. Quand on ne sait pas _____ on parle, on ne dit rien !

2. Il y a longtemps qu'on ne s'est pas vus ? _____ devenez-vous ?

3. _____ est votre opinion sur la situation économique ?

4. Dites-moi _____ vous pensez de ce projet ?

5. Je ne savais pas _____ répondre.

6. De ces deux tableaux, _____ préférez-vous ?

7. Entre ces deux experts, _____ fais-tu le plus confiance ?

8. _____ est le thème de ce roman ? De _____ il s'agit ?

B. Transpose the sentences from direct to indirect discourse.

Examples:

*Qu'est-**ce que** vous désirez ?* (direct discourse)

*Dites-moi **ce que** vous désirez.* (indirect discourse)

1. A quoi penses-tu ? Puis-je savoir _____

2. De quoi avez-vous besoin ? Dites-nous _____

3. Qu'est-ce qu'il est devenu ? Personne ne sait _____

4. Quelle sera sa décision ? Qui sait _____

5. Qu'est-ce qui le stimulait ? Je me demande _____

6. Qu'est-ce qu'il pense de ce livre ? Je n'ai aucune idée _____

2. <u>The relative pronouns</u>.

A. Complete the following sentences with relative pronouns, combining them with demonstrative pronouns if needed.

Example:

Voilà le bureau _____ on nous a indiqué.

*Voilà le bureau **qu'**on nous a indiqué.*

1. Le pays _____ je viens a changé depuis mon exil.

2. Je m'arrêterai lorsque j'aurai obtenu _____ je demande.

3. Je m'arrêterai lorsque j'aurai obtenu _____ j'ai besoin.

4. Nous ne comprenons pas bien _____ vous chagrine.

5. Il termina sa lettre, après _____ il quitta son bureau.

6. _____ vivra, verra. (proverbe)

7. Voilà un obstacle _____ nous n'avions pas pensé.

8. Il racontait son histoire à _____ voulait bien l'écouter.

9. Il prétend m'avoir averti de la situation, _____ n'est pas vrai.

10. L'ennui est une maladie _____ le travail est le remède.

B. Translate the following sentences.

Example:

He who lives by the sword shall perish by the sword.

(***Celui***) *qui vit par l'épée périra par l'épée.* (***Celui*** is often omitted in old proverbs or maxims dating way back in time).

1. What you said does not surprise me._____

2. The date when he was expected had passed._____

3. That's all I want._____

4. Don't believe a word he says._____

5. All that glitters is not gold._____

6. You who are so wise, tell me what I should do._____

3. The demonstrative pronouns.

A. Complete the following sentences with demonstrative pronouns.

Côte à Côte 2

Example:

*Le prix de l'or est plus élevé que **celui** de l'argent.*

1. Les défauts de _____ homme sont _____ d'un orgueilleux.

2. _____ qui se conçoit bien s'énonce clairement. (N. Boileau)

3. Elle n'est pas de _____ qui se laissent exploiter.

4. Tous _____ qui l'ont connue vous diront du bien d'elle.

5. Quel livre me recommandez-vous ? _____ ou _____ ?

6. _____ qui aime bien châtie bien. (Proverbe)

7. Pour qui sont _____ serpents qui sifflent sur nos têtes ?

   (J. Racine, <u>Phèdre</u>)

8. _____ seuls sont heureux qui savent modérer leurs désirs.

B. Translate the following sentences:

1. This gift is for you. That one is for me._____

2. Is this what you wanted?_____

3. Those are secrets we must not divulge._____

4. I hear a car, it is our guests!_____

5. A wasp's sting is less dangerous than a scorpion's._____

6. That is not what I meant._____

Jacques Bourgeacq

Chapter 5

More about pronouns

En savoir plus : Les pronoms

I. The personal pronouns:

1) Personal pronouns are among the first to learn in an introductory French class, so there is no need to reproduce the whole list here. The potential challenge is determining their place and function in relation to the verb they modify. It concerns primarily the personal pronouns in their functions as <u>direct</u> and as <u>indirect</u> objects. In general, (and as it is with nouns in a similar function), a direct object is placed <u>directly next</u> to the verb, while an <u>indirect</u> object is pushed <u>further away</u> from it:

subj.	**ind. ob.**	**dir. ob.**	**VERB**	**dir. ob.**	**ind. ob.**
Je	*te*	*le*	*donne.*		
			Donne	*le*	*moi*
Tu	*nous*	*la*	*donnes.*		
Ne	*me*	*la*	*donne pas.*		
Elle ne	*vous*	*l'*	*a pas donné.*		
Je ne	*lui*	*en*	*donne pas.*		
			Donne-lui- en.		
Il n'	*y*	*en*	*a pas.*		
Je n'	*y*		*comprends rien.*		

Note: A sentence often contains several rhythmic syntagms with a vocal stress on each last syllable: So, when **me, te, se** find themselves in such stressed position, they become **moi, toi, soi**. The same applies as well to relative pronouns **que** and **quoi**.

Examples:

*Dites-**moi**/ de **quoi**/ vous avez **peur**/.* (three syntagms: in stressed positions, <u>me</u> and <u>que</u> turn into <u>moi</u> and <u>quoi</u>)

*Ne <u>me</u> dites **pas**/ <u>que</u> vous avez **peur**/.* (two syntagms: <u>me</u> and <u>que</u> are in an untressed position and so do not change).

There is one exception in the general personal pronoun system (in an otherwise rational system): it occurs when both object pronouns are in <u>the third person and in the affirmative or interrogative form</u>. The order is then reversed. The pronunciation of **le lui**, smoother than of **lui le** may be the reason for this inversion.

Examples:

*Je **le lui** donne.* *I give **it to him/her**.* (The indirect object is now next to the verb).

***Lui** en donnes-tu ?* *Do you give **him/her some (of it)**?*

*Donne-**le-lui**.* *Give **it to him /her**.* (In a command form, the order is conform to the system)

*Donne-**lui-en**.* *Give **her/him some**.*

Note: The partitive pronoun **en** (= *of it, of them*) is always placed last in the syntactic group.

2) <u>The second challenge</u> comes with a compound verb, such as **entendre dire, faire voir, laisser faire, voir venir**, etc. English and French have two different views of such double actions that involve two different subjects in English: eg. *to have someone do something, to hear someone say something,* etc.

Examples:

I had my students sing. (*I* is the subject of the first action *had* [= prompted], and *students* is the subject of the second action: *sing*).

Now observe the French construction:

J'ai fait chanter mes élèves. (*Faire chanter* forms a single compound verb, directed on an <u>object</u>: *mes élèves*)

I <u>had</u> them <u>sing</u>. (*them* is both object of *had* and subject of *sing*; = I prompted them to sing).

Je les <u>ai fait chanter</u>. (*les* is object of *ai fait chanter*)

To sum up, we have the impression that English analytically divides the action into two separate steps: two verbs, two subjects: *I* and *students*. In contrast, French casts a synthetic view (*faire chanter*) with one simple object, *les*, that receives the action. It is as if the subject *Je* claimed ownership of the whole process!

Another example:

I saw <u>him</u> do it. (*I* = subject of *saw*; *him*, object of *saw*, and at the same time <u>subject</u> of *do it*).

Je <u>le lui ai vu faire.</u> (*Je* = subject of *ai vu faire*; *le lui* = objects of this compound verb).

II. <u>The possessive pronouns</u>:

Let us stress again the difference between pronoun and adjective: an adjective *accompanies* a noun, while a pronoun *replaces* it. So there are two classes of possessive words:

<u>The adjectives</u>: *mon, ma, mes/ ton, ta, tes/... son, sa, ses/ notre, nos/ votre, vos/ leur, leurs*

<u>The pronouns</u>: *le mien, la mienne/ le tien, la tienne/... le sien, la sienne/ les vôtres, les nôtres/ les leurs*, etc.

Given that there is a quantity of these pronouns, and rather than duplicating a table that can be found in many introductory textbooks, we shall concentrate on just a few potentially problematic cases:

1) **<u>Le mien *vs.* à moi</u>**:

If I ask: *Is this car **yours**?*, this sentence can apply to two different situations:

a) I know you have a car: *Est-ce que cette voiture est* **la tienne** *?*

b) I don't know if you have a car: *Est-ce que cette voiture est **à toi** ?*

A toi indicates mere ownership, while **la tienne** contrasts two cars: the one <u>I see here and now</u>, and the one, virtual, <u>I know you own, but have not yet seen</u>.

2) There is a frequent case in English, when a possessive adjective introduces a gerund (i.e. a verb form ending in *--**ing***). This construction, impossible in French, is not expressed by a possessive adjective, but by other constructions:

<u>Examples</u>:

I appreciate *your helping* me out.

J'apprécie *l'aide que vous m'apportez*.

Your winning the lottery will change your life.

D'avoir gagné à la loterie, *cela va **vous** changer la vie*.

3) The frequent English possessive case (ending in '**s**) contrasts with the French demonstrative pronoun marking possession:

<u>Example</u>:

I received **Paul's answer** and I am waiting for **Mary's**.

*J'ai reçu **la réponse de Paul** et j'attends **<u>celle de</u> Mary***.

4) Another English construction has no exact French equivalent:

Example:

*I met a friend **of yours**.* (two French solutions)

*J'ai fait la connaissance d'**un ami à vous**.*

*J'ai fait la connaissance d'**un de vos amis**.* (suggests awareness of a number of friends)

5) The case of the definite article as possessive adjective has been treated in Chapter 1: *Levez **la** main.*

*Raise **your** hand.*

6) There is another English possessive construction that cannot be reproduced in French: The isolated possessive adjective, left alone in suspense without a preceding referent, is too vague in French, resulting in a change of structure:

***Ours** is a nation of merchants.* (isolated possessive adjective)

***Notre nation** est une nation de marchands.* (repetition)

***Nous sommes une nation** (**un peuple**) de marchands.* (= better solution)

III. The indefinite pronouns:

Many French introductory textbooks provide long lists of indefinite words, adjectives, pronouns, adverbs, with their equivalents in English. Some problematic cases can benefit from further exploration.

1. The versatile and capricious *tout*:

The word ***tout*** can assume several functions: adjective, pronoun, and even adverb.

1) as an adjective, ***tout*** varies in gender and number, and usually

precedes both the article and the noun:

*Je travaille **tous les jours**.*

*Voilà une recherche de **toute une vie**.* (of a whole life)

Without an article, the adjective ***tout*** means ***any***:

Tout** homme est mortel.* ***Any *man is mortal.*

2) As a pronoun, ***tout*** also varies in form like the adjective:

*Ils sont **tous** arrivés.* or ***Tous** sont arrivés.*

*Les candidates sont **toutes** présentes.*

***Tout** est bien qui finit bien.* (neuter gender)

3) As an adverb, and unlike other adverbs, **tout** enjoys special treatment! Unlike other adverbs, it can vary (or not vary) in gender and number:

a) Before a masculine adjective, ***tout*** is invariable:

*Il est **tout** seul. Ils sont **tout** seuls.*

b) Before a feminine adjective starting with a ***vowel*** or a mute ***h***, ***tout*** is also invariable, probably for pronounciation's sake:

*Elle était **tout** heureuse.* (= *très, complètement*)

c) Before a feminine adjective starting with a consonant, ***tout*** is variable in gender and number:

*Elle était **toute** contente.*

*Elles étaient **toutes** contentes.* (ambiguous sentence: *All of them* were *happy* or *They were quite happy*? The context should clarify).

This question of <u>agreement</u> is more important than suspected, regarding the meaning of a sentence, as just seen above:

Examples:

*Ils étaient **tout heureux** d'être invités.* (*They were **quite** happy...*)

*Ils étaient **tous heureux** d'être invités.* (***s** is pronounced; **All** of them were happy*).

This versatility of ***tout*** has also contributed to the coining of numerous adverbial phrases: ***tout de suite*** (*right away*), ***tout à fait*** (*completely*), ***tout à coup*** (*all of a sudden*), ***tout droit*** (*straight ahead*), ***tout de même*** (*just the same*), ***en tout cas*** (*in any case*), ***tout doucement*** (*very slowly*), etc.

4. The sequence of ***quelques, plusieurs, certains, des,*** meaning ***some***:

There often is confusion between the meaning of these adjectives, three of them being equivalent to the English ***some***:

Examples:

*J'ai gagné **quelques** dollars cette semaine.* (*a few*)

*J'ai vu **plusieurs** films cette semaine.* (*several*, i.e. more than one or two, but quite limited in number)

*J'ai vu **des** films ces derniers mois.* (indéfinite article plural, numerically vague)

*J'ai aimé **certains** de ces films.* (*some*, as selective and qualitative: some yes, others no!)

5. <u>The neutral indefinite words (pronouns and adverbs) modified by a qualifying adjective</u>:

For some unexplained reason, when a <u>neutral gender</u> indefinite pronoun (e.g. *rien, quelque chose, quelqu'un, personne,* etc.) connects with a qualifying adjective, it requires *de* (remember the nuisance French preposition!). And the adjective remains masculine (a <u>default</u> masculine gender, akin to neuter gender):

<u>Examples</u>:

Je n'ai **rien** *vu* **d'***intéressant.*

Connaissez-vous **quelqu'un de** *fiable ?* (*fiable* = *dependable*)

Non, je **ne** *connais* **personne de** *fiable.*

J'ai vu **quelque chose** *d'extraordinaire.*

<u>Note</u>: Even when speaking of a feminine person, **quelqu'un** retains its neuter gender. Thus we will say:

Cette femme est **quelqu'un d'**intéressan<u>t</u>. (masculine form for neuter)

The reverse is true: speaking about a man, one will say:

C'est **une personne** *intéressan***te** (the Latin noun **persona**, a mask, was feminine. Note that here *personne* is <u>not</u> an indefinite pronoun, but a full-fledged noun).

An interesting phenomenon, seldom presented in most textbooks, is the situation of some indefinite pronouns and adverbs coupled with a negation: *personne, rien, aucun, pas, point,* etc. These words originally were <u>not</u> negations at all; they became so as a result of their long association with the negation *ne*. By the time it had become Old French, the Latin negative adverb **non** had eroded to *ne*, a particle so short and inconspicuous that the need was probably felt in verbal communication to reinforce it in some way:

Examples:

*Je **ne** bougerai **pas**.* (***pas*** originally comes from Latin ***passum*** = a step, namely *I won't budge **a step***)

*Je ne vois **rien*** (***rien*** comes from Latin ***rem*** = a thing, as in ***republic***; namely *I don't see **a thing***)

*Je ne vois **personne**. I don't see **a person*** (a soul).

*On ne le voit **guère**.* (from an ancient Frankish word, ***waigaro***, meaning *much*)

And there are other words that also became negations by this form of "contagion". Aside from the first example below, they are colloquial expressions:

*Je ne sais **point** si cela est vrai.* (from ***punctum*** = a point, a dot)

*Je n'y comprends **goutte**.* (from ***guttam*** = a drop)

*Je ne mange **mie**.* (from Latin ***micam***, a crumb; now an archaic expression)

6. **Aucun**: Originally, *aucun(e)* was not a negation either. It became so with the development of the French language. Latin *alius* (other, else) + *quis/quem* (who, what) became *alquem*; then *aucun* was basically *someone* or *something else* (and <u>not</u> *no one* or *nothing* else, as it means today).

Even though all the above considerations about language history do not assist much in developing the automatisms of speaking or writing, they unveil the <u>expressive</u> dimension and the historical nature of language. It is much like researching a family DNA to determine one's roots and identity. As language is a "living" organism, whether we are aware or not of its deep workings, we cannot escape its cultural heritage when we communicate, in our own language as well as in another language.

EXERCISES

1. The personal pronouns:

A. Replace object nouns with personal pronouns:

1. J'ai vu peindre ce tableau.

2. Ne faites pas tomber ce beau vase.

3. Ne laissez pas mon mari vendre ce tableau.

4. Nous avons entendu Alice chanter cette chanson.

5. J'ai entendu Pierre parler de ce film.

6. Laissez cet enfant réciter son poème.

7. Parlez à vos collègues de votre voyage en Afrique.

B. Translate the following sentences:

1. Don't talk to me about it.

2. I'll bring it to you.

3. We will have it translated.

4. We will have her translate it.

5. I had not thought about it.

6. I am interested in her.

7. Have them view the video.

8. It is she who told me.

9. Let me do it?

2. The possessive pronouns and adjectives:

A. Complete the following sentences with possessive pronouns or adjectives.

Examples:

*Tu as **tes** ennuis et j'ai **les miens**.* (*tes* = adj. / *les miens* = pron.)

1. Chacun invoqua ses raisons, lui _____ et eux _____.

2. Cette casquette est-elle (yours) _____? (two solutions: explain)

3. Non, ce stylo n'est pas ____ : celui-là est bleu, et (mine)___ est rouge.

4. Je voudrais vous présenter un ami _____ (of mine).

5. Je voudrais vous présenter un de _____ amis. (my)

6. J'ai eu l'avis de tes frères, et j'aimerais connaître _____. (yours)

B. Translate the following sentences:

1. I received Paul's answer; I am still waiting for yours.

2. I received Paul's answer; I am still waiting for Mary's.

3. Ours is a country of immigrants.

4. I did not appreciate his calling me at three in the morning!

5. Raise your hand, if you agree.

6. The boy's mother was washing his hands.

7. The girl's mother was washing her hands.

8. His working long hours cannot last.

3. The indefinite pronouns and adjectives:

A. Equivalents of _all_ and _any_. Translate these sentences:

Examples:

All humans are created equal.

*Les humains sont **tous** créés égaux.*

***Tous** les humains sont créés égaux.*

***Every/any** man has two countries, his own and France.* (Thomas Jefferson) ***Tout** homme a deux patries, la sienne et la France.*

1. Don't give them any, they don't deserve it.

2. Do you have any questions?

3. All I need is a long vacation.

4. I expect them at any moment now.

5. Any man is mortal.

6. They had walked all day in the rain and were all wet.

7. These books, I read them all.

8. They all had arrived, some at the very last minute.

B. Indefinite, gender-neutral words modified by adjectives. Translate:

Examples:

*I have just read **something** funny.*

*Je viens de lire **quelque chose** d'amusant.*

1. Have you ever seen anything so strange?

2. Do you want anything else?

3. No, I don't want anything else.

4. I met someone interesting at the party.

5. What's new?

6. What more do you want?

7. Nothing more!

8. He did not say much more. (much = *grand-chose*)

9. He does not speak much in class. (two solutions)

C. The sequence of *quelques, plusieurs, certains, des,* meaning *some*. Complete the following sentences according to the context. (In case of multiple answers, explain them).

Example:

*Exigent comme il est, il n'aime que **certains** aliments.*

Demanding as he is, he likes only **certain** foods.

1. Je n'attends pas qu'un seul visiteur, mais _____.

2. Dans la vie on rencontre toujours _____ personnes aimables, mais il n'y a que _____ qu'on aimerait épouser.

3. Pour le déjeuner, j'ai commandé du poisson et _____ frites.

4. Je te vole _____ frites, car elles sont si appétissantes !

5. Il y a _____ jours où on aimerait rester au lit !

6. De ces pâtisseries, il y a ____ que j'aime, (others) _____ non.

Jacques Bourgeacq

Chapter 6

The expression of movement and its verbs:

semantics and syntax

L'expression du mouvement et ses verbes :
sémantique et syntaxe

I. <u>Sémantique</u>:

A. <u>Verbs of motion</u> (***to*** and ***from*** <u>a point of reference</u>):

Due to the dual meaning of the English verb ***to return***, speakers of English are often confused when it comes to choose one of several French equivalents: ***retourner***, ***revenir*** and ***rentrer***, all of which can be translated as ***to return***.

1) ***Retourner*** stands for ***aller*** again:

*Je suis **allé** à Paris cette année, et j'ai l'intention d'y **retourner** l'an prochain.*

2) ***Revenir*** means ***to come back*** (towards the speaker):

*(A Parisian friend writes me) Si tu as passé de bonnes vacances à Paris chez moi, **reviens** me voir bientôt.*

3) ***Rentrer*** basically means ***to return*** to the home departure point.

It has a dual perspective: towards home or away from home. Several examples are needed:

(I am away from home) *Il est tard. Il faut que je **rentre** me coucher.*

(A mother writes her traveling son) *Paul, **rentre** (or **reviens**) avant mon anniversaire.*

(At the movie ticket office) *Oh ! j'ai oublié ma carte de crédit, il faut que je **retourne** chez moi la chercher.*

(***rentrer*** means **return home** and stay for a while, i.e. not touch and go; so it would not be appropriate in this last situation).

B. Transportation verbs: *to bring and to take* (somewhere):

These two English verbs, sometimes troublesome even to speakers of English, can also present difficulty in choosing the French equivalents. In addition, these verbs also combine with prefixes and suffixes that complicate further the challenge.

The French language has two basic verbs to express the action of transporting or transferring something or somebody somewhere: ***porter*** for things and ***mener*** for persons.

Examples:

*Veuillez **porter** ces lettres à la poste.*

*Je vais **mener** mon enfant à l'école.*

(The emphasis is toward the expressed destinations: here the post office and the school).

The action of taking something to the speaker (***bringing***) is expressed by ***apporter*** and ***amener*** (the prefix ***a--*** comes from the Latin preposition ***ab***, meaning *to, toward*; ***ab*** turns into ***ap*** before the letter ***p***).

Examples:

*Voulez-vous m'**apporter** une bière ?*

*Vous pouvez **amener** quelques amis à notre soirée.*

(The emphasis and direction are toward the speaker)

Note: The French themselves sometimes make the error of using ***amener*** for things instead of ***apporter***!

Another prefix is commonly combined as well: ***em*** (from Latin preposition ***ex, e***, meaning *away from,* or *along with;* before the letter ***m*** the consonant is doubled):

Examples:

Emportez *ce dossier, puisque l'affaire est classée.*

(the emphasis is away from here, no matter where to)

*Le juge déclara: « **Emmenez** le prisonnier . »*

(the emphasis is away from the court; destination unimportant or obvious)

All the above verbs can also combine with an added prefix, ***re***, expressing the idea of repetition: either ***again*** or ***back***.

Example:

*Veuillez **reporter** ces livres à la bibliothèque.* (*take back, return*)

For some unexplained reason, the verb *****remener*** does not exist! **Ramener** is used instead, and illogically (!) to express the idea of *taking someone back somewhere, away from the speaker.*

Examples:

*Cet élève est parti sans demander la permission. Veuillez le **ramener***

93

à l'école. (*take back* or *bring back*, depending of where the speaker is, at the school or elsewhere?)

Le médecin a dit: « **Ramenez**-moi cet enfant dans une semaine. »

(just *bring back*, since the perspective is that of the speaking doctor)

Apporter is also combined with the prefix *re*, contracted into *r* before a vowel: ***rapporter***.

Example:

Je vous prête ce livre, mais il faudra me le **rapporter**. (*bring back* = toward me, as the speaker).

There is a second exception to an otherwise logical system: When dealing with a rather heavy object or a vehicle, the basic verb **porter** would be strange (since it also means *to carry*). So **mener** is used:

J'ai **mené** ma voiture au garage pour changer l'huile. or

J'ai **conduit** ma voiture au garage pour changer l'huile.

In none of all these examples, the verb **prendre** (= *to take*) was used, since it does not express a direction *to* or *from* a point of reference. It is simply an equivalent of to *seize, grab, take hold of,* etc.

II. Syntax:

Another category of verbs of motion need our attention, especially since they illustrate a very different perception of common situations in French and in English.

Verbs describing *modes* of movement correspond closely in meaning (semantically) in both languages: *to walk* = *marcher*; *to swim* = *nager*, *to run* = *courir*; *to drive* = *conduire*; *to fly* = *voler*, etc. Yet, each language has its own mental grasp of these processes, resulting in a very dissimilar syntactical formulation.

The French verbs listed above describe <u>only the image</u> of a specific motion, and <u>not the dynamic direction itself</u>. In contrast, English expresses in a single verb both the mode (the image) and the dynamics: unlike French, English motion verbs have what is called a ***vectorial*** aspect (the term is borrowed from geometry: a line with a direction, an arrow).

<u>Example</u>:

*I **walk** to school every morning.*

*Je **vais** à l'école **à pied** tous les matins.*

<u>Note</u>: *Je marche à l'école* is a perfectly good French sentence, but it means something else: *I walk **inside** (on the premises of) the school*, <u>not **to, toward**</u> the school. (The same for: *J'ai conduit à Chicago,* which means: *I drove **within the city limits** of Chicago,* <u>not **to**</u> Chicago).

The impossibility to use the verb ***marcher*** (or *conduire*) in these situations calls for some explanation. English tends to express movement from a <u>sensorial and chronological perspective</u>, in the order in which the action unravels; French, on the other hand, seems to view first the situation as a whole and then rearranges it in <u>an order of importance</u> (rather than chronologically and visually): first the action (*je vais*) and afterwards the mode (*à pied*). The linguists J. P. Vinay and J. Darbelnet (<u>Stylistique comparée du français et de l'anglais</u>) called these two modes of perception: "<u>plan du réel</u>" for English and "<u>plan de l'entendement</u>" for French (ie. sensorial perception vs. mind mapping). This is another example of an *analytical* mental process (cf. the place of adjectives, Values, #3).

The <u>real</u> French verbs of movement, those that are *vectorial,* are the ones void of a sensorial image: *aller, venir, retourner, revenir, sortir, partir,* etc. They are simple "arrows" of motion.

<u>Examples</u>:

*She **drove bac**k home. Elle **est rentrée (revenue)** en voiture.*

*He **flew across** the Atlantic. Il **a traversé** l'Atlantique **en avion**.*

Nothing, however, keeps us from saying: *Il a **volé** au-dessus de l'Atlantique*, since in this sentence **voler** is not used with a stated destination (it is here <u>non-vectorial</u>). Now we can say, also appropriately, the following:

*Il **a volé** au-dessus de l'Atlantique **jusqu'à** Paris.*

(Here the vectorial function is assumed by the préposition *jusqu'à*).

Correct also is the sentence:

*Je **marchais** <u>vers </u>l'école, lorsque j'ai vu un accident.*

(The preposition **vers** assumes here the <u>vectorial function</u>; like a discharged battery, the preposition <u>*à*</u> appears to have lost over the centuries its original dynamic force; it was "diluted" indeed after having acquired many other meanings and functions in the language).

The very image of the motion may even at times be totally omitted in French, if the context makes it obvious and thus unnecessary.

<u>Examples</u>:

(inside a home) *She **walked over** to the window.*

*Elle **s'approcha** de la fenêtre.*

In this context, there is no need in French to specify the nature of the movement. It is obvious that under normal circumstances one does <u>walk</u> inside a home. So only the idea of the English adverb, ***over*** (i.e. the direction), is expressed in French: ***s'approcha***. It is as if the French speaker expected (unconsciously of course) the <u>listener</u> to form in one's own mind the image that the English language delivers explicitly, on a silver platter, to the listener!

*The leaves were **blown away** by the wind.*

*Les feuilles étaient **emportées** par le vent.*

(The idea of *blowing* being obvious, it is omitted).

EXERCISES

1. Verbs of motion (*to* and *from* a point of reference): ***Revenir, retourner, rentrer.* Complete the sentences according to the situations.** Explain if there are multiple answers.

<u>Examples:</u>

(At a party) *Oh, il est déjà 3 heures du matin ! Il faut que je **rentre** chez moi.*

1. Une maman écrit à sa fille qui est à Paris : « Ma chère Marie, _____. Paris est trop dangereux aujourd'hui . »

2. Mon séjour en Floride a été merveilleux. J'aimerais bien y _____ l'an prochain.

3. Un ami vous écrit de France, où vous avez passé l'été : « Quand _____ -tu nous voir ? »

4. Votre père, voyant le plaisir que vos vacances à Cancun vous ont procuré, vous propose : « Puisque tu t'es tant amusée là-bas, je te paie un autre voyage. Veux-tu y _____ ? »

5. Invité chez quelqu'un, au moment de se séparer, votre hôte vous dit : « Surtout, il faut _____ nous voir . »

6. Oh zut ! J'ai oublié ma carte de crédit chez moi, il faut que je _____ la chercher. Attends-moi un moment, je reviens.

7. Ses parents l'autorisent à sortir le soir, à condition qu'il _____ avant minuit.

8. Un camarade vous lit une lettre qu'il vient de recevoir de France : « André demande quand tu vas _____ à Paris pour passer un autre été dans sa famille . »

2. **Transportation verbs** (*to bring* and *to take*): **Porter, mener, prendre** and their derivatives (*reporter, ramener, emporter*, etc.). **Complete the sentences according to the following situations.** Explain if there are multiple answers.

Example:

Portez *cette lettre à la poste.*

Take *this letter to the post office.*

1. Ce matin, j'ai _____ mon fils chez le médecin.

2. N'oublie pas de _____ ta guitare à notre soirée.

3. N'oublie pas de _____ ta sœur à notre soirée.

4. Quand elle est allée en Europe, elle ne _____ qu'une seule valise.

5. Je veux bien vous _____ au cinéma, mais je ne peux pas rester avec vous; il faut que je _____, j'ai du travail en retard.

6. Il a eu l'amabilité de me _____ en ville avec lui.

7. Il s'approcha du bureau, _____ le document qui était dessus, et disparut sans bruit.

8. Veux-tu _____ ce livre pour moi à la bibliothèque ?

9. Vous voyez ce livre sur l'étagère. Veuillez le_____, je ne veux plus le voir ici !

10. (à votre père, collé devant un match à la télévision) : « Papa, veux-tu me _____ à la bibliothèque, cela ne te _____ que quelques minutes. »

11. Puisque tu vas voir ce film, pourrais-tu me _____ avec toi ? Je veux le voir aussi.

12. _____ cet enfant à ses parents, et dites-leur de mieux le surveiller à l'avenir.

13. _____ -moi cet enfant dans une semaine, et faites en sorte qu'il _____ ses médicaments régulièrement.

14. (au bureau) Ah, si vous allez en ville, voulez-vous me _____ un sandwich au jambon, je vous prie ? Et _____ -en un pour vous aussi, c'est moi qui invite.

15. Je vous prête ce livre, mais il faudra me le _____.

Jacques Bourgeacq

Chapter 7

The Indicative mood and its verb tenses:

perspectives and aspects

Le mode indicatif et ses temps verbaux :
Perspectives et aspects

<u>The notion of mood</u>: As a refresher, it may be useful to explore briefly the notion of ***mood*** as a linguistic term. As a general grammatical term ***mood*** refers to the <u>attitude</u> of the speaker (or sometimes of a person alluded to) toward the situation being presented. It is not to be confused with the separate notion of ***tense***, which refers to the *time* of this situation. Both English and French have several *moods*, usually (but not exclusively) expressed by verbs, to characterize an action or a process: *the indicative, subjunctive, imperative, conditional and infinitive moods.*

In this chapter, we concern ourselves with the ***indicative mood***. In the indicative mood, the action or process is viewed as being or having been real, factual, or projected as such into the future. The concordance between things outside our consciousness and our thinking process <u>does not even come into question</u>. The given is that we simply *"say it like it is."*

I. <u>The perspectives and aspects of verbs</u>:

When viewed from the now moment, our mind cuts time into three "slices:" present, past and future. In these three time slots, actions can be viewed from different *perspectives* and *aspects*, the combination of which ultimately determine which **tense** to use.

The *perspective* (or angle of vision) is the point in time from which the speaker views the action: from the now moment, or from a moment in the past or in the future.

The *aspect* relates to the "fabric," the substance of the action itself: is the action in progress? is one of its limits, beginning or end, situated? Is the action presented as a block, in its totality? Or as a repetitive series?, etc. Here are the types of *aspects*:

Punctual: The action is felt as just a point, a dot in time, void of any duration.

Global: The action is grasped in its totality, from beginning to end.

Initial: (or **inchoative**) The action is pinpointed in its beginning only.

Terminative: The action is pinpointed in its end only.

All the above aspects apply to actions that can be located (pinpointed) in time, and usually require for past actions a *passé composé* or a *passé simple*. (If any of these limits is felt, the *imparfait* tense is impossible!).

Durative: (or **imperfective**) The action is viewed from within, from a point during its unraveling, without a thought for its beginning or end. (It is like arriving late at the movies!). For past actions, the tense used is then the *imparfait*.

Iterative (or **habitual**): The action is viewed as repetitive or habitual, as a series of the same process, usually without any concern for its beginning or end. (In a way, it is a form of the durative aspect).

These last two aspects apply to an action or series of an action that, viewed at a given moment (i.e. the perspective), is not mentally situated in its beginning or its end. When viewed from a past perspective, the action is expressed by the *imparfait*.

In any given situation, and as we have already said above, **the combination of both the perspective and the aspect will determine the *tense* to be used.**

The method presented here may seem more complex than it really is. After some practice, it soon becomes familiar and very reliable. It also helps penetrate the "psychology" of the time-worlds of French and English. What ultimately needs to be developed is a "gut feeling" for the system, so that eventually the right tense comes to mind instinctively.

If generations of English speakers studying French have been struggling with French verb tenses, it is because the often simplistic rules presented traditionally in many textbooks worked only part of the time, leaving students confused. The notoriously troublesome difference between the *passé composé* and the *imparfait* is a case in point! And this confusion occurs because English does not always distinguish between these two tenses by using systematically its existing devices (*was...-ing, kept...-ing, used to, would,* etc.) to stress aspects, while French must obligatorily select one or the other aspect and tense.

II. The verb tenses:

1. Le présent :

The present tense poses little problem, as the perspective of the message coincides exactly with that of the action. It might be useful to note that the present time is a fleeting instant between past and future, considered as a fixed point in time only for convenience. (Some linguists and philosophers even deny the very existence of a present!).

An important detail is seldom mentioned in grammar books: <u>The present tense always has a **durative** (**imperfective**) aspect</u>, the very same aspect in fact as the *imparfait*. Indeed, when we express a current action, it has already begun (otherwise we would not be aware of it), and it continues to unravel as we speak. However, the *present tense* also poses little problem, since it does not have to compete with other tenses, like the past tenses (*imparfait, passé composé, plus-que-parfait, passé simple*). Since every time we present an action happening right now it is already in existence, our focus is fixed <u>only</u> on a point situated <u>within</u> its unraveling. Its beginning and its end are totally out of the picture.

Examples:

*Il **boit** une bière.*   *He **is drinking** a beer.* (durative)

*Il **boit** (en ce moment).*   *He **is drinking**.* (durative);

*Il **boit**.   He **drinks**.* (can be iterative, habitual; he may be an alcoholic!)

*Il **boit** une bouteille de vin **le dimanche**.* (iterative, habitual)

It is possible to stress the now moment, if desired, by an added precision: ***en train de*** + infinitive:

*Il est **en train de** boire une bière.* (durative)

2. <u>L'imparfait</u> :

The imperfect tense has the ***durative*** (***imperfective***) aspect, <u>exactly as the present tense</u>. What does change is just the perspective: our mind is now centered back into the past ***inside the action***, and focused on a specific instant of its unraveling, ignoring totally its beginning and its end (though we may already know the end of the story, but at that very moment we are <u>focused only</u> on that specific instant).

Examples:

*Il **pleuvait** quand je **suis arrivé** à la gare.*

(*pleuvait* = durative: no limit indicated, as the rain was already falling when I arrived and it kept falling)

(*suis arrivé* = punctual or initial: the beginning of the action is located)

Let us consider another similar situation:

*Il **pleuvait** quand j'**arrivais** à la gare.*

Now the tense of both verbs is ***imparfait*** (not only are they *durative*, but also *iterative*. The situation is indeed repetitive, habitual. Here, **quand** means that <u>whenever</u> (<u>each time</u>) I arrived at the station, it was already raining (as the rain had not waited for me to start and keep falling!). The recurring rain is viewed from within the series of its occurrences, without a thought for its limits. What makes it *durative* (*imperfective*) and *iterative* is the complete mental lack of limits: the beginning and the end of each rain and of the whole series of rains are irrelevant here. Facing this type of presentation, though, the reader is left in suspense, with a feeling of incompleteness, waiting for a <u>real event</u> to be presented with a verb in the ***passé composé*** (or ***passé simple***), that will situate firmly the action at a specific point in time. It can be said that the *imparfaits* set the background stage while the *passés composés* or *passés simples* move the story forward.

The ***imparfait*** is ideal to present a situation in which the narrator is or appears to be ***re-living*** an experience, as it ***was happening*** in the past, <u>not</u> as it ***did happen*** as an event. The ***imparfait*** is indeed a tense frequently used by narrators to enlist the reader's imagination and absorb him/her into the story.

3. Le passé simple :

This tense receives much less attention in the typical classroom than other past tenses, since it is most often replaced by the *passé composé* in daily verbal exchanges. The ***passé simple*** is generally reserved for literary or historical writing. Both tenses, however, can have *the same aspects*, though not always the same perspective, as we shall see later.

<u>Examples</u>:

Il *pleuvait* quand j'***arrivai*** à la gare.

The *aspects* are the same as the previous first example above (cf. the *passé composé*, previous section). What has changed is the perspective. The passé simple is a **real** past tense, in that the writer's perspective is totally detached from the now moment (unlike the *passé composé*, as we shall see in the next section): with the *passé simple* the speaker's mind is **totally** focused back into time. The *passé simple* is sometimes called *passé historique,* due precisely to this perspective.

The *imparfait* can be (or not), just as "historical" (i.e. used in a historical text) as the *passé simple*, depending on the perspective of the sender of the message, but it has a different aspect, as we saw.

The *passé simple* can take all aspects, except *durative* (*imperfective*), since it always expresses a time limit.

Examples:

Il **partit**. (punctual)

Il **cria** *trois fois.* (global, superseding iterative, as a complete, limited action)

Il **dormit** *pendant 3 heures.* (global aspect, the duration is limited)

Il **s'assit** *à son bureau et* **travailla** *jusqu'à minuit.* (initial and terminative, each verb presented in its own limit)

4. Le passé composé :

This tense is actually a "hybrid" of present and past. Its basic equivalent in English is the *present perfect*. As in English, the *passé composé* often describes actions begun in the past and continuing in the present.

Example:

*J'***ai cherché** *la vérité toute ma vie.* (the search began in the past and comes up to the present, and may keep going into the future)

I **have searched** (or **been searching**) *for truth all my life.*

However, in daily informal exchanges, the *passé composé* has replaced the *passé simple* over time, and now it often corresponds to the past tense (*preterit*) in English:

Example:

*Hier, **j'ai cherché** mes clés toute la journée.* (global aspect and not reaching the present)

*Yesterday, I **looked** for my keys all day.*

One may wonder why and how the *passé composé* turned out to replace almost exclusively the *passé simple* in verbal communication. It appears that the gradual switch occurred in the 17th-18th centuries. The most plausible reason is that in daily life, we frequently talk about topics, past situations, and events that remain relevant to us. They may also tend to be a bit too mundane for history… The *passé simple* has gradually been reserved for events far remote in time or requiring a more elevated style, such as literary and historical writing.

The next two examples will help measure and feel the main difference between these two tenses:

*Napoléon **écrivit** le code civil français.* (passé simple)

*Napoléon **a écrit** le code civil français.* (passé composé)

The *passé simple* presents the writing of the Napoleonic code as a purely historical event, an action completely detached from the present, done and over with.

The *passé composé* presents the writing of that same code as a past event whose effects are still felt in the present. As a matter of fact, the Napoleonic code is still relevant, as it remains in force today in France.

To help measure clearly the difference between the *passé composé* and the *imparfait*, let us compare these two examples:

1) *Quand **je suis entré** dans la salle, tous mes étudiants **riaient**.*

*When I **entered** the room, all my students **were laughing**.*

(durative aspect: *laughing* already in progress)

2) *Quand je **suis entré** dans la salle, tous mes étudiants **ont ri**.*

*When **I entered** the room, all my students **laughed**.* (initial aspect: = began laughing).

The <u>perspective</u> is from the past in both situations. The narrator's mind is focused back into time on a point from which to view the unraveling of the situation. But the <u>aspects</u> are different, as follows:

a) ***je suis entré***: initial or punctual aspect. It is an action viewed from that limit, thus the *passé composé*.

b) ***riaient***: durative (or imperfective) aspect. The action is grasped from inside its progression, ignoring limits, thus the *imparfait*. The action can only be a mere coincidence: No cause and effect possibility.

c) ***ont ri***: the laughter ***began*** at, or immediately after my entrance: initial aspect, thus *passé composé*. Furthermore, a cause and effect relation is sensed as a strong possibility: I may have been wearing a funny hat, causing people to laugh!

5. <u>Le plus-que-parfait</u> :

The perspective of the *plus-que-parfait* is <u>always</u> a point in the past. This tense always presents an action that occurred <u>prior to that past perspective</u>. The question of aspects in the case of the *plus-que-parfait* seems to have little bearing on the situation (though it is possible to identify them).

<u>Examples</u>:

*Hier, quand je **suis arrivé** chez lui, il **était** déjà **sorti**.*

*Chaque fois que j'**arrivais** chez lui, il **était** déjà **sorti**.*

Whether *punctual* or *iterative* (*habitual*), the time relation between the verbs in both situations is the same: One action had occurred before the other took place and often continued...

6. Le futur :

The perspective is obvious: a projection from the present ahead into time. The question of aspect seems of lesser importance, since there are only two tenses for actions projected in the future: the simple ***futur*** and the ***futur antérieur*** (future perfect). They are similar to English usage, except for one detail, as shown in this example:

Quand j'arriv<u>erai</u> chez lui, il m'attendra à la porte.

When I **arriv<u>e</u>** at his home, he **will be waiting** at the door.

In this type of sentence (with *when* and other conjunctions of time), English often uses the *present tense* in the subordinate clause. By contrast, French uses the future tense in the main and subordinate verbs, when the action is projected into the future.

<u>A special case</u>: The future tense can sometimes be used to replace a present tense, in order to stress <u>probability</u>. It then has a ***modal*** value.

<u>Example</u>:

*Je ne vois pas de lumière chez lui. Il **sera** en voyage.*

I don't see any light in his home. He **is probably** traveling.

(Here, the future tense projects into the future a <u>present</u> evaluation <u>that will be verified or confirmed as fact</u> at a later time; hence the modal value of probability).

7. Le futur antérieur :

This tense is used exactly as in English. The perspective and aspects are the same as for the *plus-que-parfait*, though projected ahead in time, instead of back into the past.

*Quand j'**arriv<u>erai</u>** chez lui, il **sera** déjà **parti**.*

When I **arrive** at his home, he **will** already **have left**.

(Again, observe the *present tense* in English after **when** to express a future action).

The futur antérieur can also be used in the main clause, thus corresponding to an English present perfect.

<u>Example</u>:

After I **<u>have</u> done** my homework, I **will go** see a film.

*Après que j'**<u>aurai</u> fini** mon devoir, j'**irai** voir un film.*

<u>Note</u>: We are leaving out a discussion on the **passé antérieur** tense, as it is highly unlikely that English speakers get to use it. It is related in form and usage to the *passé simple* and strictly literary (written). Simply learn to recognize it in texts.

<u>Example</u>:

*Après qu'il **eut payé** l'addition, il **sortit** du restaurant.*

After he **had paid** the bill, he **left** the restaurant.

Or simply:

After **paying** the bill, he **left** the restaurant.

8. <u>One last item before concluding this chapter</u>:

There is another aspect in verbs, that is used less frequently: the **permanent aspect**. It occurs in situations of a timeless or endless nature. Its tense is always the **present**, called **omni-present**.

<u>Examples</u>:

*J'**ai appris** à l'âge de 4 ans que la terre **<u>tourne</u>** autour du soleil.*

(*tourne* = permanent aspect of a natural phenomenon)

We may, however, choose another aspect and perspective in the same situation.

Example:

J'ai appris à l'âge de 4 ans que la terre **tournait** *autour du soleil.*
(*tournait*: imperfective aspect)

In this last example, the ***imparfait*** adds a stylistic nuance: The emphasis is now focused on the <u>instant of discovery</u> in the experience of the child, leaving aside temporarily the eternal nature of the situation.

The ***permanent aspect*** is often found in proverbs, truisms, maxims, etc.:

Example:

On ***a*** souvent ***observé*** que la fin **justifie** les moyens.

Note: In spite of the *past perspective*, the verb ***justifie*** remains in the present tense. Wouldn't it be nice if only this situation belonged in the past?

EXERCISES

1. Analyze the use of verb tenses in this text. In particular, analyze the contrast made by the journalist between the passé composé and the passé simple.

This is a newspaper article about an event in the life of the famous writer Jorge Luis Borges, who at that time lived in Europe.

Jorge Luis Borges (86) se marie et annonce qu'il

« ne retournera jamais en Argentine ».

Il y a quelques années, pour mieux se débarrasser de lui, une revue nationaliste argentine **avait annoncé** que Jorge Luís Borges n'**existait** pas. Pour une fois, cette « fiction » n'**était** pas due à l'écrivain argentin, qui toute sa vie, n'**aura cessé** de surprendre et d'égarer ses lecteurs, ses amis comme ses ennemis.

On **vient** d'apprendre, sans commentaires, que Borges, qui **est** âgé de quatre-vingt-six ans, **a épousé** sa secrétaire Maria Kodama. En même temps, de Genève où il **s'est établi** depuis quelques mois, il **a fait** savoir qu'il « ne **retournerait** jamais en Argentine », et il **a décidé** de vendre l'appartement qu'il y **possède**.

« Buenos Aires n'**est** plus la ville où j'**ai vécu**. Il y **avait** en elle une passion qui **a disparu** : la passion littéraire et la métaphysique. » L'auteur de *L'Aleph* **se sent** bien en Europe et particulièrement à Genève où il **vécut** entre 1914 et 1918, où il **fit** ses études secondaires et **passa** son baccalauréat. C'**est** donc dans la ville de son adolescence qu'il **a décidé** une fois encore d'étonner en se mariant. (Le Monde, mai 1986)

*(For the following exercises, you may wish to use the **passé composé** in cases that would normally call for a **passé simple**).*

2. Complete the following text with verb tenses dictated by the context. If at times several options are possible, point them out. Identify the other elements (e.g. adverbs) in the text that facilitate the choice of tenses.

This excerpt is from the novel La Peste by Albert Camus. Events are expressed in the passé simple, but the passé composé can be used for a text resembling a chronic. Expect also the need to use imparfaits at times... Be vigilant!

Le surlendemain, le docteur Rieux (rentrer) _____ chez lui de bonne heure. Un télégramme l'(attendre) _____ et lui (annoncer) _____ la nouvelle de la libération définitive de la peste. Quelle immense joie (détendre) _____ ses nerfs ! Il (aller) _____ donc pouvoir recommencer. Pendant quelques instants il ne (pouvoir) _____ dire un seul mot. Enfin il (appeler) _____ sa mère et, à son entrée, il (s'apercevoir) _____ qu'elle (avoir) _____ l'air inquiète. Elle lui (expliquer) _____ alors que son ami Tarrou ne (se sentir)

_____ pas très bien et qu'il (montrer) _____ les symptômes de la peste. A ces mots, Rieux (se rendre) _____ immédiatement dans la chambre de son ami. Celui-ci (être) _____ étendu sur le lit et (recevoir) _____le docteur avec un faible sourire qui en (dire) _____ long. Rieux (comprendre) _____ tout de suite que son ami (savoir) _____ qu'il (attraper) _____ la peste. Cependant tout espoir ne pas (être) _____ perdu et Rieux (se prépare) _____ immédiatement à livrer pour Tarrou son ultime combat contre la peste qui, en dépit de tous les efforts du docteur ne pas (aller) _____ tarder à emporter sa dernière victime. (Albert Camus, *La Peste*, ©Éditions Gallimard. 1947. Tous les droits d'auteur de ce texte sont réservés. Sauf autorisation, toute utilisation de celui-ci autre que la consultation individuelle et privée est interdite. www.gallimard.fr)

3. Same exercise as the preceding one.

This is an excerpt from Anatole France's La vie littéraire. *It presents a historical celebrity, the Prince of Bismarck, who after retiring from politics relives in retrospect his* past *political life. In restituting the text, bear in mind that the past is presented in two "layers" of time.*

Vingt ans plus tard, dans une heure intime et solennelle, il (sentir) _____ lui monter au cœur l'épouvante et l'horreur de son œuvre. Ce (être) _____ à Varzin. Le jour (tomber) _____. Le prince, selon son habitude, (être) _____ assis après son dîner, près du poêle, dans le grand salon où (se dresser) _____ la statue de Rauch : « la Victoire distribuant des couronnes. » Après un long silence, pendant lequel il (jeter) _____ de temps à autre des pommes de pin dans le feu et (regarder) _____ droit devant lui, il (commencer) _____ tout à coup à se plaindre de ce que son activité politique ne lui (valoir) _____ que peu de satisfaction et encore moins d'amis. Personne ne le (aimer) _____ pour ce qu'il (accomplir) _____. Il ne (faire) _____ par là le bonheur de personne, ni de lui-même, ni de sa famille, ni de qui que ce fût.

Quelqu'un lui (suggérer) _____ qu'il (faire) _____ celui d'une grande nation. -- Oui; mais le malheur de combien ?, (répondre) _____-il. (A. France, <u>La vie littéraire</u>, Calmann-Lévy, 1933)

4. Same exercise as the preceding ones. Explain if there are multiple answers. (Watch out: The final verbs may be tricky!)

This text is an excerpt of André Gide's early novel Isabelle. *It is a conventional narrative, with in the middle a passage in direct discourse.*

Quand je (arriver) _____ à la station de Breuil-Blangy, la nuit (être) _____ à peu près close. Je (être) _____ seul à descendre du train. Une sorte de paysan en livrée (venir) _____ à ma rencontre, (prendre) _____ ma valise et me (escorter) _____ vers la voiture qui (stationner) _____ de l'autre côté de la gare. L'aspect du cheval et de la voiture (couper) _____ l'essor de mon imagination : on ne (pouvoir) _____ rêver rien de plus minable. A l'intérieur, une odeur de poulailler suffocante... Je (vouloir) _____ baisser la vitre de la portière, mais la poignée me (rester) _____ dans la main. Il (pleuvoir) _____ dans la journée; la route (être) _____ tirante : le cheval (peiner) _____ aux montées, (trébucher) _____ aux descentes et parfois, tout inopinément, il (stopper) _____. --Du train dont nous (aller) _____, (penser) _____-je, nous (arriver) _____ au Carrefour longtemps après que mes hôtes (se coucher) _____. Je (avoir) _____ grand faim; ma bonne humeur (tourner) _____ à l'aigre. Je (essayer) _____ de regarder le pays : sans que je m'en fusse aperçu, la voiture (quitter) _____ la grande route et (s'engager) _____ dans une route plus étroite et beaucoup moins bien entretenue; les lanternes ne (éclairer) _____ de droite et de gauche qu'une haie continue, touffue et haute; elle (sembler) _____ nous entourer, barrer la route, s'ouvrir devant nous à l'instant de notre passage, puis aussitôt se refermer.

(André Gide, *Isabelle*, ©Éditions Gallimard. 1911. Tous les droits d'auteur de ce texte sont réservés. Sauf autorisation, toute utilisation de celui-ci autre que la consultation individuelle et privée est interdite. www.gallimard.fr)

Chapter 8

The subjunctive mood: hypothesis and subjectivity

Le mode subjonctif : hypothèse et subjectivité

Much has been said to define the French **subjunctive mood**, that it expresses actions or ideas "contrary to fact", "doubt or uncertainty," all sorts of "emotions" (fear, desire, wish, etc.), "judgment," etc. All these statements are partly true, but none of them can explain <u>alone</u> the basic principle that lies at the root of the *subjunctive mood*, and encompasses all the above explanations.

Regarding the *indicative mood*, we had stated earlier that "the concordance between things outside our consciousness and our thinking process does not even come into question." It is a given. Now with the **subjunctive mood**, we enter a very different world, one in which whatever the speaker or writer expresses is ***filtered*** through his/her **subjective** attitude. He/she projects the message as *one's own perception*, rather than as an outside, objective reality or fact, independent of the onlooker. The fact that most speakers may not be conscious of this subjective process does not exclude its dynamic existence. Throughout the centuries, many languages, from Greek to Latin and other Romance languages, have seen the world, in turn, through these two distinct "lenses." Once again, this phenomenon can be explained as culture expressing itself through the minds of its members, whether <u>aware or not</u> of the process. Walking up or down a slope, we are not necessarily aware of the resulting mechanical forces of physics, but they are here at work!

Note: This mind/language connection has been convincingly described by American linguists, George Lakoff and Mark Johnson, in Metaphors we live by, The University of Chicago Press, 2003.

While statements in the indicative mood can be expressed directly in a main clause, the *subjunctive statement* is most often expressed in a subordinate clause, which depends on a main clause that determines its nature: is it objective reality or subjective thought? In fact, the very word *subjunctive* means in Latin *"joined under,"* (i.e. the subjunctive clause is indeed a dependent clause).

Examples:

*Vous **êtes** en bonne santé. J'en suis content.* (The statement of good health is in the main clause --> indicative)

*Je suis content que vous **soyez** en bonne santé.* (The statement of good health is in the dependent clause --> subjunctive)

Note that the second example does not deny any fact (and apparently, this fact is no news to the speaker). The real and main message expressed here is: *Je **suis** content*, and it is indeed in the indicative mood. The second statement: *que vous **soyez** en bonne santé*, is presented as a mere element of my (subjective) contentment as speaker, and as such it is in the *subjunctive* mood. This might be a selfish attitude, but it may also be seen as expressing more vividly my sharing in someone else's good fortune!

One will occasionally encounter a verb in the subjunctive mood without a stated main clause, such as "***Vive** la reine !*" or "(***Que***) la paix **soit** avec vous.*" These subjunctive clauses depend on an understood (unexpressed) main clause, such as: "***Je souhaite que...***," "***Je désire que...***" *(wish, desire)*.

The subjunctive mood exists in English, but it seems of lesser importance and usage than the French subjunctive. To the extent that using verbs in the subjunctive in daily speech in English may appear intellectually uppity to the listener (at least in the United States), it is not the case in French, as all kinds of French people will use it on a daily basis, though perhaps less frequently than in the past (until the 19th century). Since then, two of the subjunctive mood tenses have even become rare: the *imparfait* and *plus-que-parfait*. For the remaining two thriving tenses, the **present** and the **passé**, there are many cases in which the subjunctive mood is automatic, grammatically and socially obligatory.

I. The obligatory subjunctive:

As an obvious expression of subjectivity, the subjunctive must be used:

1) after a main verb expressing **will, command, necessity**: *vouloir, demander, dire, permettre, proposer, il faut*, etc.

Examples:

***Dites**-lui qu'il **vienne** vite.* (dire = demand: indirect command)

*Il **faut** qu'il **vienne** vite.* (necessity)

***Dites**-lui que je **suis arrivé** et qu'il **vienne** me voir.*

(**Dire** and some other declarative verbs (*demander, prier, exiger*, etc.) can have two distinct meanings: *to inform* or *to command*, requiring either indicative or subjunctive moods respectively).

2) after a main verb expressing a **sentiment**: *aimer, craindre, désirer, être content, préférer, souhaiter, regretter*, etc.

Examples:

*Nous **regrettons** qu'il ne **soit** pas **venu**.*

*Je **suis heureux** que vous **soyez** en meilleure santé.*

3) after a conjunction expressing *futurity* in a subjective perspective: **avant que, en attendant que, jusqu'à ce que**, etc., (but not *après que*, followed by the indicative mood, since it is expressing a past objective reality).

Example:

*Il restera à son poste **jusqu'à ce qu'on le remplace**.* (subjunctive)

*Il est parti **après qu'on lui a payé** son dernier salaire.* (indicative)

Note: Unlike the English conjunctions <u>until</u>, <u>till</u>, **jusqu'à ce que** <u>cannot</u> be used after a negative verb: it cannot express <u>the absence of an action</u>.

Compare:

*Attendez-moi **jusqu'à ce que** je revienne.*

***Ne** commencez **pas** le travail **avant que** je revienne.*

(Both sentences can use **until** in English)

4) after a conjunction expressing **purpose**: **afin que, pour que, de peur que, de façon que, de sorte que**, etc.

Example:

Conduisez lentement, ***de sorte qu'on puisse*** vous suivre. (= so that, in order that)

Note: If **de sorte que** expresses a <u>consequence</u> rather than a purpose, the indicative mood is used.

Example:

*Elle a beaucoup étudié, **de sorte que** ses notes **sont** maintenant excellentes.* (consequence = factual result)

*Elle a beaucoup étudié, **de sorte que** ses notes **soient** excellentes.* (purpose, intention; but no indication the grades are so)

5) after a conjunction expressing **concession**: **bien que, quoique, quoi que, malgré que,** etc.

Example:

Quoi que vous ***disiez***, je ne vous crois pas. (*Whatever you **may** say...*; a subjective, hypothetical statement)

6) after a conjunction expressing a **hypothetical condition**: *à condition que, à supposer que, en supposant que, pourvu que,* etc.

Example:

*A **supposer que** tu **aies gagné** à la loterie, que ferais-tu ?*

7) after a conjunction expressing **restriction**: *sans que, à moins que,* etc., expressing uncertainty.

Example:

*Nous ferons un pique-nique, **à moins qu'il (ne) pleuve**.* (the chance of rain is pure speculation)

Note: *Ne* is optional and not a "real" negation in this construction. It will also appear in subjunctive clauses with ***de peur que, de crainte que, avant que***. *Ne* is perhaps used here as an afterthought, a wishful psychological "incantation," a mental dismissal of the event considered, as in **No rain, please! Cross your fingers!**

Regarding its treatment of *mood*, the English language seems to make no distinction between the cases below, which remain in the ***indicative mood*** or ***form***:

I think he **is** courageous.

I don't think he **is** courageous.

Do you think he **is** courageous?

By contrast, in order to show the importance of the main clause in French as a determinant of the mood, let us observe the equivalent French sentence presenting the very same situations as above:

Je pense qu'il est courageux.

Je pense qu'il n'est pas courageux.

The positive judgment (*penser*) coincides with the information (*courageux*) and thus can be sensed as reality, as well as the negative statement: no courage!

On the other hand, in the phrase: *Je ne pense pas qu'il soit courageux,* what the main clause begins by denying cannot simply be stated as reality. Hence the subjunctive mood *soit*.

Next example:

Pensez-vous qu'il **soit** courageux ?

The question indicates a subjective attitude of uncertainty, and thus the situation is best expressed in the subjunctive mood. The indicative is not impossible here, however: it may then indicate that the speaker strongly believes the person **is** in fact courageous, and wants to know the listener's opinion. This subtle case leads us to the next segment of our discussion: the *optional* subjunctive mood.

But before proceeding to the next section, here is a final comment regarding the lesser use of the subjunctive mood in English.

1) There are no permanent, uniquely special conjugated subjunctive forms in modern day English; the subjunctive is expressed by "borrowed" forms from other moods and tenses (*were, might, would, be, the absence of an s in the 3rd person*, etc.):

Examples:

I wish I was... (*was* is a past tense; as well as the more correct *I wish I were...*)

God save the king (the absence of an **s**, showing it is not indicative)

He explained it, so that I would learn it well. (conditional form **would**)

*So **be** it! (__not__ so it **is**)*

2) It is as if, in English, <u>the main verb interacted with the language form itself</u>, instead of the thought underlying it.

<u>Examples</u>:

*I believe she **is** here.*

*I don't believe she **is** here.* (No change of mood in spite of a denial; if one does not believe it, why say "she **is** here?"). Different languages, different logic...!

II. <u>The optional subjunctive</u>:

A given statement may at times have two distinct meanings, and may thus require different moods:

1) *Je cherche un restaurant qui **soit** près d'ici.*

*Je cherche un restaurant qui **est** près d'ici...*

In the first sentence, the restaurant is a figment of my imagination, some wishful hope for convenience. In the second sentence, I know the restaurant does exist in reality, but where is it? I am looking for its location, which I have forgotten.

2) *C'est la plus grande maison que j'**ai** visitée.*

*C'est la plus grande maison que j'**aie** visitée.*

In the first case, the situation is stated as a simple fact. The basic sentence is: *J'ai visité la plus grande maison* (among other houses), emphasizing its size with a highlighting syntax: *C'est... que.*

The second case is presented as a subjective view, a judgment meaning: *In my opinion, it is (or might be) the largest (ever)...*

3) Someone in serious religious doubt may well ask a clergyman:

***Croyez-vous** qu'il y **ait** un Dieu ?*

The subjunctive mood expresses uncertainty: maybe yes, maybe no; or doubt, or even a question asked as a challenge.

A clergyman, on the other hand may ask his congregation:

***Croyez-vous** qu'il y <u>a</u> un Dieu?*

The indicative mood is used here, since the clergyman insists on stating it as a <u>*fact*</u>, and wants to know if his audience is of the same mind. It means: Do you believe <u>as I do</u>... The clergyman thinks that "*Certaines personnes ne croient pas qu'**il y a** un Dieu*," as he does. (indicative mood)

4) The subjunctive mood tends also to be used in sentences introduced by a <u>superlative adjective</u>:

<u>Example</u>:

C'est le **meilleur** film que *j'aie vu* cette année.

(definitely a subjective judgment).

But: *C'est le format de ce livre **le plus grand** que j'ai acheté.* (indicative mood: a factual statement about comparing several formats or editions; it is just an emphasized construction of: *<u>J'ai acheté</u> le plus grand format de ce livre*).

5) With respect to *emphatic constructions*, the French use many **impersonal phrases**. They are main cues presenting situations viewed either as <u>objectively real</u> or <u>subjectively sensed</u> (below is a partial list):

Il est possible que... (subjective --> subjunctive)

Il est probable que... (projected as likely real--> indicative)

Il est impossible que... (denied --> subjunctive)

Il est peu probable que... (viewed as unlikely --> subjunctive)

Il est clair que... (if clear, potentially real --> indicative)

Il n'est pas clair que... (if not clear, unlikely --> subjunctive)

Il semble que... (50/50%, subjective --> subjunctive)

*Il **me** semble que...* (Against the logic of the system, this phrase usually requires the indicative mood!).

III. Verb tenses in the subjunctive mood:

The *verb tense* used in the dependent (i.e. subordinate) clause *depends* on its time relation with the main clause. The dependent verb can express an action occurring <u>before</u>, <u>during</u> or <u>after</u> the main verb. The two sets of examples below will present the various situations. The factual and the judgmental situations are placed in parallel for better clarity.

1) The perspective is <u>the present</u> for the first double set:

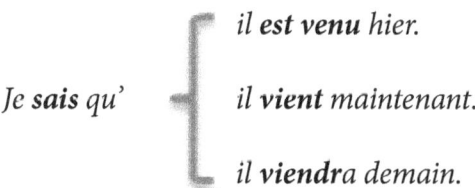

*Je **sais** qu'* { *il **est venu** hier.*
*il **vient** maintenant.*
*il **viendra** demain.* }

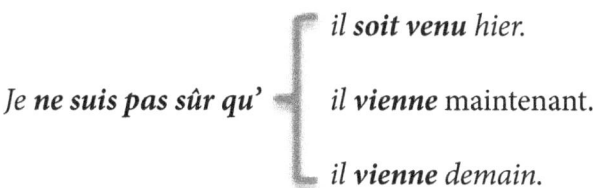

*Je **ne suis pas sûr** qu'* { *il **soit venu** hier.*
*il **vienne** maintenant.*
*il **vienne** demain.* }

We observe that the verb tenses are the same in both the factual and the judgmental situations, with one exception: <u>The subjunctive mood has no special form for the future tense</u>, and so it uses the present tense.

2) Observing now these same situations from a past perspective:

Je **savais** qu'
- il **était venu** la veille.
- il **venait** à ce moment-là.
- il **viendrait** le lendemain.

Je **n'étais pas sûr** qu'
- il **soit venu** la veille. (**fût venu**: literary)
- il **vienne** à ce moment-là. (**vînt**: literary)
- il **vienne** le lendemain. (**vînt**: literary)

<u>Note</u>: The literary forms are those of the subjunctive *plus-que-parfait* and *imparfait*. These literary tenses are used only in elevated style, and mainly in the third person singular, as shown above. As for the *conditional* **viendrait**, here it is an **indicative tense** (a future viewed from a past perspective: *would, was to come*), <u>not</u> the *conditional mood* that we shall discuss in the next chapter.

4. Alternatives to the indicative and subjunctive moods:

When the main and dependent verbs share the same subject, the construction can often be favorably simplified with an infinitive verb, thus avoiding the choice of one of the two moods.

<u>Example</u>:

Devant ce spectacle de la nature, **je** *crois que* **je** *rêve !*

--> *Devant ce spectacle de la nature,* **je** *crois* **rêver** *!*

Before this natural display, **I** think **I** am dreaming!

Je *suis content* **d'être** *ici avec toi.*

I am glad I am here with you.

(The other construction, *Je... que je...*, would be awkward here in French.

Conclusion:

This chapter should have erased, or at least diminished the impression that the *subjunctive mood* is mainly a subtle game for the intellectually inspired or elitist French speaker. It is rather a sort of built-in mental "lens," through which the world outside our mind is experienced. The interplay of these two moods, indicative and subjunctive, can be a constant source of increased and expressive nuances. We hope the subjunctive mood is no longer as complicated and scary as it is often expected by beginning and intermediate learners of French.

EXERCISES

I. Identify the verbs in the subjunctive mood, and those in the indicative mood, and explain why they are used. *This is an excerpt from Blaise Pascal's* Pensées. *The author exhorts his 17th century readers to reflect on the insignificant status of man in the universe.*

Disproportion de l'homme. Que l'homme **contemple** donc la nature entière dans sa haute et pleine majesté; qu'il **éloigne** sa vue des objets bas qui l'**environnent**. Qu'il **regarde** cette éclatante lumière, mise comme une lampe éternelle pour éclairer l'univers, que la terre lui **paraisse** comme un point au prix du vaste tour que cet astre **décrit** et qu'il **s'étonne** de ce que ce vaste tour lui-même n'**est** qu'une pointe très délicate à l'égard de celui que les astres qui **roulent** dans le firmament **embrassent**.

Mais si notre vue **s'arrête** là, que l'imagination **passe** outre; elle **se lassera** plutôt de concevoir que la nature de fournir. Tout le monde visible n'**est** qu'un trait imperceptible dans l'ample sein de la nature. Nulle idée n'en **approche**. Nous **avons beau enfler** nos conceptions au-delà des espaces imaginables, nous n'**enfantons** que des atomes, au prix de la réalité des choses. C'**est** une sphère infinie dont le centre **est** partout, la circonférence nulle part. Enfin c'**est** le plus grand caractère sensible de la toute-puissance de Dieu, que notre imagination **se perde** dans cette pensée.

Que l'homme, étant revenu à soi, **considère** ce qu'il **est** au prix de ce qui **est**; qu'il **se regarde** comme égaré dans ce canton détourné de la nature; et que de ce petit cachot où il **se trouve**, j'**entends** l'univers, il **apprenne** à estimer la terre, les royaumes, les villes et soi-même à son juste prix. Qu'**est**-ce qu'un homme dans l'infini ? (B. Pascal, Pensées, 1669)

2. Complete the text with verbs in the subjunctive or indicative moods, as required by the context. Identify and explain possible options.

This is an excerpt from an open letter by Aimé Césaire, an author from Martinique, explaining why he broke away from the communist party. He speaks here for the African and Caribbean societies of the 1930s.

Nous voulons que nos sociétés (s'élever) _____ à un degré supérieur de développement, mais d'elles-mêmes, par croissance interne, par nécessité intérieure, par progrès organique, sans que rien d'extérieur (venir) _____ gauchir cette croissance, ou l'altérer ou la compromettre.

Dans ces conditions, on (comprendre) _____ que nous ne (pouvoir) _____ donner à personne délégation pour penser pour nous, délégation pour chercher pour nous : que nous ne (pouvoir) _____ désormais accepter que qui que ce (être) _____, fût-il le meilleur de nos amis, (se porter) _____ fort pour nous.

Je (croire) _____ en avoir assez dit pour faire comprendre que ce ne (être) _____ ni le marxisme ni le communisme que je (renier) _____ , que ce (être) _____ l'usage que certains (avoir) _____ fait du marxisme et du communisme que je (réprouver) _____. Ce que je (vouloir) _____, ce (être) _____ que le marxisme et le communisme (être) _____ mis au service des peuples noirs, et non les peuples noirs au service du marxisme et du communisme. Que la doctrine et le mouvement (être) _____ faits pour les hommes, non les hommes pour la doctrine ou pour le mouvement. Et bien entendu, si je (être) _____ chrétien ou musulman, je dirais la même chose.

(A. Césaire, Présence africaine, October 1956)

3. Same exercise as the preceding one. Indicate which mood is used with verbs that do not change forms.

This is an excerpt from a 20th century novel by Marguerite Yourcenar: Mémoires d'Hadrien. In a letter to his grandson, the Roman emperor states here his position on slavery...

Je (douter) _____ que toute la philosophie du monde (parvenir) _____ à supprimer l'esclavage : on en (changer) _____ tout au plus le nom. Je (être) _____ capable d'imaginer des formes de servitude pires que les nôtres, parce que plus insidieuses : soit qu'on (réussir) _____ à transformer les hommes en machines stupides et satisfaites, qui (se croire) _____ libres alors qu'elles (être) _____ asservies, soit qu'on (développer) _____ chez eux, à l'exclusion des loisirs et des plaisirs humains, un goût du travail aussi forcé que la passion de la guerre chez les barbares. A cette servitude de l'esprit, ou de l'imagination humaine, je (préférer) _____ encore notre esclavage de fait. Quoi qu'il en (être) _____, l'horrible état qui (mettre) _____ l'homme à la merci d'un autre homme (demander) _____ à être soigneusement réglé par la loi. J'ai veillé à ce que l'esclave ne (être) _____ plus cette marchandise anonyme qu'on (vendre) _____ sans tenir compte des liens de famille qu'il (se créer) _____, cet objet méprisable dont un juge ne (enregistrer) _____ le témoignage qu'après l'avoir soumis à la torture, au lieu de l'accepter sous serment. J'ai défendu qu'on le (obliger) _____ aux métiers déshonorants ou dangereux, qu'on le (vendre) _____ aux tenanciers de maisons de prostitution ou aux écoles de gladiateurs. Que ceux qui (se plaire) _____ à ces professions les (exercer) _____ seuls : elles ne (être) _____ que mieux exercées. (Marguerite Yourcenar, *Mémoires d'Hadrien*, ©Éditions Gallimard. 1951. Tous les droits d'auteur de ce texte sont réservés. Sauf autorisation, toute utilisation de celui-ci autre que la consultation individuelle et privée est interdite. www. gallimard. fr)

4. Rewrite or speak each time this same sequence: "*Mes parents /venir/la semaine prochaine,*" using the following cues and the appropriate mood (subjunctive or indicative):

Je crois, je ne crois pas, je veux, je ne veux pas, il est possible, il est probable, il est peu probable, il n'est pas impossible, il n'est pas improbable, espérons, je n'espère plus, je suis content, je ne suis pas content, je m'attends à ce que, il faut, il ne faut pas, cela me chagrine, ça ne m'étonne pas, je doute, je ne doute pas.

Examples:

Il n'est pas certain *que mes parents* **viennent** *la semaine prochaine.*

Il est certain *que mes parents* **viendront** *la semaine prochaine.*

5. Translate the following sentences.

Examples:

*She left **without** my **knowing** it. = Elle est partie **sans que** je le **sache**.*

*I worked **until** I had finished the project. = J'ai travaillé **jusqu'à ce** j'aie fini le projet.*

1. Whatever he may have done, I will forgive him.

2. She left her instructions, so that I <u>would not</u> make a mistake.

3. She left her instructions, so that I <u>did not</u> make a mistake.

4. Don't start until I come back.

5. Unless you have an objection, I'll serve myself a cocktail.

6. He will not quit his job, for fear he may not find another one.

7. I will not leave before I receive your message.

8. Supposing you had inherited a fortune, would you retire?

9. So long as you let me know in advance, I can step in for you.

10. While we wait for them to come, let's have a drink.

11. Whether you want it or not, tuition will increase.

12. I was not sure she had received my email, and was willing to accept my offer.

13. Are you happy you received this award?

14. I don't believe I heard your name.

15. Will you call me before you leave?

Jacques Bourgeacq

Chapter 9

The conditional mood: hypothesis and unreality

Le mode conditionnel : hypothèse et irréel

Viewing a condition:

There are two distinct ways of viewing a condition: one is to project the action as real, possible, achievable (if met); the other is merely conjecturing or speculating on an unlikely or impossible situation (as if "for the heck of it!").

Examples:

*Demain, s'il ne **pleut** pas, nous **ferons** un pique-nique.*

(indicative mood, since the weather forecast is for fair skies)

*Demain, s'il ne **pleuvait** pas, nous **ferions** un pique-nique.*

(conditional mood, since the weather forecast is for possible or probable rain. Sorry no picnic. Just wishful thinking. Would have been nice...)

Note: The strange use of the *imparfait* (in the indicative form) in the second example is explained below.

Origin of the conditional form:

Latin had no special mood for presenting "unreality," no so-called "conditional" mood. A hypothetical situation was expressed by the subjunctive mood. There was no special verb form for actions depending on a condition or viewed as unreal or unachievable. Philologists (language historians) tell us that in the third century, new forms began to appear in the Empire, composites of the Latin *infinitive* and the auxiliary verb *habere* (*to have*). It is evident, at first glance, that the endings of the modern future and conditional verb tenses closely resemble the present and imperfect forms of *avoir* (*habere*): *-ai, -as, -a, -(av)ons,* etc. and *-ais, -ais, -ait, (av)ions,* etc. The Latin syntax being very flexible, the verb *habere* was often placed after the infinitive, and eventually stuck to it as an integral part of the verb; roughly: *aimer* + *(av)ais* --> <u>*aimerais*</u> for the conditional. Soon, the same process applied to a <u>newly-coined future tense</u> (different from written Latin: *ama<u>bo</u>, ama<u>bis</u>,* etc. = I *will* love, you *will* love, etc.): *aimer* + *(av)ai* --> **aimerai**. And the modal meaning of the verb *habere* = **to have to** + infinitive (i.e. obligation or necessity) gradually faded away, retaining only the idea of future.

<u>Note</u>: A similar process exists in the development of the English language with the *modal form* **will** (*to want, desire*) and **shall** (*to owe, must*), derived from ancient English verbs. Let us observe a couple of examples in modern English, that show an occasional survival of the <u>modal</u> meaning: **Will you sit down?** or I **will not do** that. The verb **will** here is <u>modal</u>, still expressing the idea of *will, desire*, and not a mere prediction in the future. The French equivalents are: <u>**Voulez**</u>-**vous vous asseoir ?** and **Je ne <u>veux</u> pas faire cela.**

The same evolution affected other verbs, like **devoir, pouvoir, savoir, faire,** etc. which also combined with the infinitive. But perhaps because of their length (two syllables) and their uniquely individual and strong modality, these verbs retained their place, before the infinitive root and detached from it. **Aller** + infinitive is another way of expressing futurity, especially immediate futurity. Similarly, **venir de** + infinitive expresses a very recent past: Je **vais** bientôt <u>arriver</u> chez moi. / Je **viens** juste <u>d'arriver</u> chez moi.

Note: Near future and recent past come from the **present tense** used with both verbs, *aller* and *venir de*. They are actually present tense with mental projections into the future or the past.

As alluded in the preceding chapter, the ***conditional*** can be either a ***mood***, with its two tenses. Or the term can also refer to a ***tense of the indicative mood*** (in which case the term ***conditional*** is a misnomer, since no condition is involved). A more exact term might be: "future viewed from the past," or "retrospective future."

I. The conditional mood:

1. The *si* clauses:

The conditional mood is used principally to speculate on a situation that is believed to be contrary to fact or unlikely. It is often introduced by the subordinating conjunction *si* (= *if*). Against any logical reason, the verb in the *si clause* is in the indicative mood (as if it were a reality), while the main verb is, appropriately, in the conditional mood. The switch from a subjunctive to an indicative form in the *si-clause* seems to have occurred during the 12th century, after a period of alternation. The similar endings of the ***conditional present*** and the ***indicative imparfait*** may have facilitated that change (maybe?).

Examples:

a) In the perspective of the present:

*Aujourd'hui s'il **faisait** beau, je **ferais** une promenade.*

(But alas the weather is bad; **si** + indicative imparfait and conditional present)

b) In the perspective of the future:

*Demain s'il **faisait** beau, je **ferais** une promenade.*

(But the weather may not cooperate; same tenses as in the present perspective)

c) <u>In the perspective of the past</u>:

*Hier, s'il **avait fait** beau, j'**aurais fait** une promenade.*

(But the weather was bad; so much for the promenade; **si** + plus-que-parfait and conditional past. In this perspective, both are <u>compound tenses</u>: plus-que-parfait and conditional past, expressing a situation that could have been but was not).

A condition in the past can have consequences in the present or the future. In that case, the main verb can change to express it:

<u>Examples</u>:

*Si j'**avais** mieux **étudié** dans ma jeunesse, j'**aurais** maintenant un meilleur emploi.*

*Si tu **avais eu** ton permis de conduire l'été dernier, tu **pourrais** maintenant aller à l'université en voiture.*

All things considered, the conditional mood is very similar in English and French. The main challenge is learning the forms.

2. **The "polite" conditional**:

The conditional mood can be used instead of the indicative to soften a demand or a command.

<u>Example</u>:

-- *Que désirez-vous ?*

-- *Je **veux** une limonade.* (a little brusque)

-- *Je **voudrais** une limonade.* (a more polite formula)

The second reply is more polite, because it implies an unspoken but culturally-felt condition, such as: "*if you **were** so kind as to serve me one*," "*si vous **étiez** assez aimable pour m'en servir une.*" This subtle, considerate manner of placing the decision in the listener's court is extremely frequent in French society. And English often uses a conditional form in similar situations:

I would like... I'd rather..., same as *"Please," "If you please."*

3. The conditional mood as an alleged statement:

The conditional is also used in statements that need further verification, as <u>a condition to achieving certainty</u>.

<u>Example</u>:

*Selon des sources non-officielles, la paix **serait** signée.*

(the conditional present ***serait*** replaces the indicative present ***est***, as it suggests a precondition: *"if this piece of news were to be confirmed"*).

<u>In English</u>: *According to unofficial sources, peace **is allegedly** signed.*

II. <u>The conditional as a tense of the indicative mood</u>:

This so-called conditional expresses <u>*no hypothetical condition*</u>. It merely presents a future action viewed retrospectively from a past perspective.

<u>Examples</u>:

We will say in the present moment:

*Elle ne **sait** pas encore **si** elle **viendra** à la réunion.*

If we present this very same situation tomorrow in retrospect:

*<u>Hier</u>, elle ne **savait** pas encore **si** elle **viendrait** à la réunion.*

In this case, ***si*** is a synonym of ***whether or not***. It is not the ***si*** = ***if*** that introduces a condition. It presents instead an <u>alternative</u>, not a condition.

<u>Note</u>: The historically common origin of the conditional mood and the future tense seems to suggest why the conditional has become a tense of the indicative mood.

Here is another example without *si*:

*Il m'a écrit qu'il **arrivera** dimanche.*

He **wrote** me he **will arrive** on Sunday

*Il m'**avait** écrit qu'il **arriverait** dimanche.*

He **had written** me he **would arrive** on Sunday. (= *was to arrive*)

This **conditional <u>tense</u>** is frequently found in novels and short stories, that narrate from a past perspective and project actions into what was then the future.

III. <u>Alternate means of expressing condition</u>:

1) Other subordinating conjunctions also express a condition: *à condition que, à supposer que, en supposant que*. They normally introduce a verb in the <u>subjunctive mood</u>, a vestige from Latin:

<u>Examples</u>:

A condition que *vous m'**aidiez**, j'accepte ce travail.*

En supposant que *vous **soyez** pauvre, **penseriez**-vous la même chose ?*

2) Unlike the above conjunctions, the conjunction ***au cas où*** (= *in case*) requires the <u>conditional</u> mood:

*Au cas où vous **auriez** besoin de moi, n'hésitez pas à m'appeler.*

<u>A final note</u>:

A vestige of the old Latin subjunctive can also be found in the

Spanish language, that generally uses the subjunctive mood in *si* clauses that are contrary to fact. French has also preserved this usage in presenting past situations. Still frequent until the 18th century, this usage is now reserved for literary style, and primarily in the third person singular.

Examples:

Si nous **avions continué** à marcher, nous **aurions pu** voir la mer.

Si nous **eussions continué** à marcher, nous **aurions pu** voir la mer.

*If we **had kept** walking, we **could have** seen the sea.*

(The first verb in the second French sentence is a subjunctive **plus-que-parfait**; nobody would ever use it now in daily conversation, or perhaps a rare purist in search of stylistic prestige!).

EXERCISES

1. Complete this text with verbs in the proper moods and tenses. (Not all verbs will be in the conditional mood. Be vigilant. The verse rhythm can be helpful in selecting the verb forms, as "alexandrin" verses have 12 syllables).

This poem is a fragment of Romantic poet Alfred de Musset, whose theme is the secret love... The conditional mood is well suited to describe a contrary-to-fact situation: "if I told you, but I do not and will not..." The paradox is that Musset does reveal here the secret!

A Ninon

Si je vous le disais pourtant, que je vous (aime) _____,
Qui sait, brune aux yeux bleus, ce que vous en (dire) _____ ?
L'amour, vous le savez, (causer) _____ une peine extrême ;
C'est un mal sans pitié que vous plaignez vous-même ;
Peut-être cependant que vous m'en (punir) _____.
Si je vous le disais, que six mois de silence

(Cacher) _____ de longs tourments et des vœux insensés :
Ninon, vous êtes fine, et votre insouciance
Se plaît, comme une fée, à deviner d'avance;
Vous me (répondre) _____ peut-être : « Je le sais. »
Si je vous le (dire) _____ qu'une douce folie
A fait de moi votre ombre, et m'(attacher) _____ à vos pas :
Un petit air de doute et de mélancolie,
Vous le savez, Ninon, vous rend bien plus jolie;
Peut-être (dire) _____-vous que vous n'y croyez pas.

Si je vous le disais, que j'(emporter) _____ dans l'âme
Jusques aux moindres mots de nos propos du soir :
Un regard offensé, vous le (savoir) _____, madame,
(Changer) _____ deux yeux d'azur en deux éclairs de flamme;
Vous me (défendre) _____ peut-être de vous voir.

Si je vous le disais, que chaque nuit je (veiller) _____,
Que chaque jour je (pleurer) _____ et je (prier) _____à genoux;
Ninon, quand vous (rire) _____, vous savez qu'une abeille
(Prendre) _____ pour une fleur votre bouche vermeille;

Si je vous le disais, peut-être en (rire) _____ -vous.
Mais vous n'en saurez rien. Je viens, sans rien en dire,
M'asseoir sous votre lampe et causer avec vous;
Votre voix, je l'entends; votre air, je le (respirer) _____;
Et vous pouvez douter, deviner et sourire,
Vos yeux ne verront pas de quoi m'être moins doux.
[...] (A. de Musset, <u>Poésies nouvelles</u>, 1937)

2. Same exercise as the preceding one. Complete this text with verbs in the proper moods and tenses.

1. *This excerpt is the conclusion of Voltaire's* Candide ou l'optimisme, *an 18th century satire directed to philosophical optimism. Henceforth, the protagonists are revealed in their new useful roles, rather than as mere pawns in a cause and effect world.*

Toute la petite société entra dans ce louable dessein ; chacun se mit à exercer ses talents. La petite terre rapporta beaucoup. Cunégonde était à la vérité bien laide ; mais elle devint une excellente pâtissière ; Paquette broda ; la vieille eut soin du linge. Il n'y eut pas jusqu'à frère Giroflée qui ne rendît service ; il fut un très bon menuisier, et même devint honnête homme ; et Pangloss disait quelquefois à Candide : « Tous les événements sont enchaînés dans le meilleur des mondes possibles ; car enfin, si vous (had not been) _____ chassé d'un beau château à grands coups de pied dans le derrière pour l'amour de Mlle Cunégonde, si vous (had not been submitted) _____ à l'Inquisition, si vous (had not run) _____ l'Amérique à pied, si vous (had not given) _____ un bon coup d'épée au baron, si vous (had not lost) _____ tous vos moutons du bon pays d'Eldorado, vous (would not eat) _____ ici des cédrats confits et des pistaches. -- Cela est bien dit, répondit Candide, mais il faut cultiver notre jardin.

(Voltaire, Candide, *1759)*

2. *The following excerpt is from a poem written in 1915 for Louise de Coligny-Châtillon by Guillaume Apollinaire, who imagines his death on the front during World War II.*

Si je mourir) _____ là-bas sur le front de l'armée

Tu (pleurer) _____ un jour ô Lou ma bien-aimée

Et puis mon souvenir (s'éteindre) _____ comme meurt

Un obus éclatant sur le front de l'armée

Un bel obus semblable aux mimosas en fleur

Et puis ce souvenir éclaté dans l'espace
(Couvrir) _____de mon sang le monde tout entier
La mer les monts les vals et l'étoile qui passe
Les soleils merveilleux mûrissant dans l'espace
Comme font les fruits d'or autour de Baratier

Souvenir oublié vivant dans toutes choses
Je (rougir) _____le bout de tes jolis seins roses
Je (rougir) _____ ta bouche et tes cheveux sanglants
Tu ne (vieillir) _____ point toutes ces belles choses
(Rajeunir) _____toujours pour leurs destins galants
(Guillaume Apollinaire, <u>Ombre de mon amour</u>, Genève, 1947)

3. The conditional as a tense: Translate the following sentences.

<u>Examples</u>:

She tells me she **will** not **come** to class today. (present perspective) = *Elle me **dit** qu'elle ne **viendra** pas en classe aujourd'hui.*

She **told** me she **would** not **come** to class today. (past perspective) = *Elle m'**a dit** qu'elle ne **viendrait** pas en classe aujourd'hui.*

1. I knew the plane had left and would arrive on time.
2. I had heard he spoke French and would seek a job as a translator.
3. I did not think she would have retired so soon.
4. I would like you to help me.
5. I did not know until this morning if I could attend today's meeting.
6. Wouldn't you rather have a glass of wine?
7. I wish he would not talk so loud.
8. I would never have believed he would do such a thing!

Chapter 10

Problematic Semi-auxiliary verbs: devoir, pouvoir, savoir, vouloir, and verb tenses

Verbes semi-auxiliaires problématiques : devoir, pouvoir, savoir, vouloir et les temps verbaux

Thinking of French <u>auxiliary verbs</u>, **avoir** and **être** come to mind first, since they have been so closely related to <u>all</u> other verbs, to such an extent that they have become an integral and permanent part of the verb form itself. Compound tenses of all verbs, such as *passé composé, plus-que-parfait, conditionnel passé,* etc., are systematically coupled with either *avoir* or *être* in their conjugations. When attached to the verbs they support, the verbs *avoir* and *être* have lost much of their original semantic meaning of *having* (= *possessing*) and *being* (= *existing*).

Semi-auxiliary verbs (also called **modal** verbs) are those that <u>occasionally</u> are coupled with another verb to place it in a certain light, called **modality**, such as *desire, obligation, necessity, possibility, capability, knowledge,* etc.:

<u>Examples:</u>

*I work, I **can** work, I **must** work, I **want** to work,* etc.

*Je travaille, je **peux** travailler, je **dois** travailler, je **veux** travailler, je **sais** travailler,* etc.

In English as well as in French, these *modal* verbs reflect the attitude of the speaker (or a protagonist referred to) towards the action being presented. However, English and French have different constructions, and sometimes different meanings. This creates some confusion for the student, who must develop new mental habits in expressing these modalities. The objective of this chapter is to survey the *semi-auxiliary verb* system, as consciously or not the French mind **thinks** *it*. We shall focus on four problematic *semi-auxiliary* verbs that are used frequently: **devoir, pouvoir, savoir** and **vouloir**.

These auxiliary verbs are used in all tenses, at times with variations in meaning depending on the context. When used in simple tenses (*indicatif présent, imparfait, futur, passé simple,* and *conditionnel présent*), as well as in the subjunctive present, the constructions in English and French do coincide. However, with compound tenses (*passé composé, plus-que-parfait, conditional past,* etc.), the situation becomes more complicated, as English and French view the matter differently. The context plays an essential part on the meaning of these modal verbs as they are actualized in a sentence.

I. Tenses and variations in meaning:

The *perspective* and *aspects* system, described in Chapter 7, applies fully to semi-auxiliary verbs. Examples are presented below, each followed by brief explanations:

1) **Pouvoir**: This verb has several meanings, depending on the situation: *can, may, to have the ability, the permission, etc.*

Examples:

Il **peut** *obtenir son diplôme.*

(*can*, has the ability; imperfective aspect, i.e., no set limits)

Cet enfant **peut** *sortir le soir.*

(*may*, is allowed to; imperfective, iterative, or habitual aspects, depending on the context)

*Il **pouvait** obtenir son diplôme.*

(just a potentiality; imperfective aspect; no indication if he did or not)

*Cet enfant **pouvait** sortir le soir.*

(had a permanent permission; imperfective or iterative aspect; no indication if he did it or not)

*Il **a pu** obtenir son diplôme.*

(managed to, succeeded in; terminative aspect)

*Il **pourrait** obtenir son diplôme, si...*

(could now or later, depending on...; imperfective aspect, and a condition)

*Il **aurait pu** obtenir son diplôme, mais...*

(could have in the past; a potential, but suggests that he did not obtain it).

2) **Devoir**: This verb has several meanings, depending on the situation: *must* (obligation, necessity), *must* (probability, likelihood), and also planning: *is to.., was to...*

Examples:

*Il **doit** étudier pour ses examens.*

(*must, has to*; imperfective aspect; almost a command; also *plans to*, depending on the context)

*Il **devait** étudier pour ses examens.*

(just necessity/obligation: *had to*; imperfective or iterative aspect, no indication whether he did or not)

*Il **devait** étudier pour ses examens, mais...*

(planning: *he was to, had planned to*; suggests he may *not have studied*)

*Il **a dû** étudier pour ses examens.*

(obligation/necessity; *did study* because *he had to*; global aspect, action took place)

*Il **a dû** étudier pour ses examens.*

(probability: *must have studied, probably studied*; global aspect)

*Il **devrait** étudier pour ses examens.*

(*should, ought to*, now or later; imperfective aspect; a piece of advice, not a firm command)

*Il **aurait dû** étudier pour ses examens.*

(*should have, ought to have*; suggests that he did not, and it's now too late!).

3. **Vouloir**: Depending on the tense, the basic meaning of this verb (*to want*) can be extended from a wish to an action, an attempt.

Examples:

*Le prisonnier **veut** s'échapper.*

(*wishes, wants*; imperfective aspect)

*Le prisonnier **voudrait** s'échapper.*

(same as situation above; *would like to...*; lesser desire, subject to a condition: e.g. but there are too many obstacles)

*Le prisonnier **voulait** s'échapper.*

(wanted, kept wanting; past perspective, imperfective aspect; just a desire, a potential; no action indicated)

Le prisonnier **a voulu** s'échapper, mais il a vite été capturé.

(initial aspect: the desire turned into an action, an attempt: tried to, attempted to escape)

Le prisonnier **aurait voulu** s'échapper.

(would have liked to...; past perspective; implies that no action followed the wish)

4. **Savoir**: The basic meaning of *knowing* can sometimes extend to *capability* and *success*, depending on the tense.

Examples:

Je **sais** nager.

(a skill, know how, can; present tense, imperfective aspect)

Note: Je **peux** nager is possible, but it would not indicate a skill; but rather the absence of a physical impediment, such as a broken leg in a cast, or the absence of danger in the water, etc.

Je **savais** déjà nager à l'âge de 4 ans.

(imperfective aspect: skill already achieved by the time indicated: at age four)

J'**ai su** nager à 4 ans.

(past perspective: à 4 ans; initial aspect: here J'ai su means I learned, acquired the skill)

Je **saurais** nager si je n'avais pas peur de l'eau.

(mere supposition in the present, subject to a condition; implying but I don't...)

II. The syntax of the modal verb:

We may have noticed in <u>all</u> the above examples that in the French compound tenses (*passé composé, plus-que-parfait, past conditional*), the modal verb + infinitive combination had a <u>different construction</u> from the one in English. Although French allows both constructions, it is usually ***the auxiliary verb that assumes the time function***, while in English it is the ***infinitive verb*** that performs this function.

<u>Compare</u>:

*He <u>must</u> **have forgotten** our meeting.*

(the modal verb *must* is in the ***present*** tense, while *have forgotten* is a ***past*** infinitive, which has the role of expressing the tense)

*Il <u>a dû</u> **oublier** notre réunion.*

(the modal verb *a dû* is in the ***past*** tense, while the infinitive *oublier* stays in the ***present*** tense)

<u>Note</u>: *Il **doit** avoir oublié notre réunion* is indeed a possible construction, but is much less frequent. So are all modal combinations.

A general rule: In past actions, the French modal verb will usually be presented <u>*from a past perspective*</u>, while the English perspective will be <u>the present</u>. The French language seems <u>to *emphasize the modality,* within which the main action (i.e. the infinitive) is inscribed</u>.

EXERCISES

1. <u>Pouvoir</u>: Complete the following sentences with a form of this verb, using the moods and tenses needed by the context.

(Analyze the context carefully. Several solutions may at times be possible. Explain.).

<u>Example</u>:

*I **could have gone** to the movies that evening, but I **had** a* *composition due the next day.*

*J'**aurais pu aller** au cinéma ce soir-là, mais j'**avais** une composition à remettre le lendemain.* (Note the different constructions)

1. Si j'ai accepté cette tâche, c'est que je _____ la mener à bien.

2. Je _____ te remplacer, si seulement tu me l'avais demandé.

3. Je ne pense pas qu'il _____ payer toutes ses dettes avant longtemps.

4. Si on m'avait chargé de ce projet, je ne _____ le faire mieux que vous.

5. Je croyais qu'on _____ aborder ce sujet en sa présence, mais je m'étais trompé

6. Je _____ enfin lui proposer d'épouser notre cause, et je crois l'avoir convaincu.

7. Même si elle _____ arriver à l'aéroport à temps, elle ne serait pas partie à cause de la grève.

8. Elle était un peu en retard. Espérons qu'elle _____ arriver à la gare avant le départ du train.

2. <u>Devoir</u>: Same exercise as the preceding one. (Analyze the context carefully).

<u>Examples</u>:

*Il n'était pas à la descente d'avion; il **a dû manquer** sa correspondance.* (probability)

He **did not get off** the plane; he **must have missed** his connection.

*Comme il **a été arrêté** pour excès de vitesse, il **a dû payer** une forte amende.* (obligation)

As he **was stopped** for speeding, he **had to pay** a big fine.

1. Je _____ assister à la réunion, mais j'ai eu un empêchement à la dernière minute.

2. Vous _____ vraiment lui écrire dès que possible. D'ailleurs, à votre place je l'aurais déjà fait.

3. Je vais à l'aéroport pour chercher mon ami, qui _____ arriver dans une heure.

4. Elle _____ rentrer, car je vois de la lumière chez elle.

5. Elle _____ être de retour, car je vois de la lumière chez elle.

6. Ce _____ être lui qui arrive : je reconnais le bruit de ses pas.

7. Je me rendais à la conférence qui _____ commencer à dix heures, lorsque j'ai été bloqué dans un embouteillage. Puis je _____ attendre une demi-heure avant de pouvoir trouver un espace pour me garer. Inutile de vous dire que je suis arrivé au milieu de la conférence.

3. <u>Vouloir</u>: Same exercise as the preceding one:

<u>Examples</u>:

*Il n'a pas **voulu** venir.* (= actually did <u>not</u> come because *he didn't want to*)

*Il ne **voulait** pas venir* (= *was refusing* to come; unkown if he eventually did or not come)

He did not **want** to come

1. Il _____ bien se joindre à notre groupe, mais sa timidité l'en empêchait. (two possibilities)

2. Aussitôt qu'il entendit prononcer son nom, il _____ s'enfuir.

3. Si j'étais à votre place, je (ne pas) _____ accepter cet emploi.

4. Si j'avais été à votre place, je (ne pas) _____ accepter cet emploi.

5. Lorsque j'avais besoin d'un service, je n'avais qu'à l'appeler, et il _____ bien venir à mon aide.

6. Même si j'avais su la nouvelle, je (ne jamais) _____ vous l'annoncer.

4. <u>Savoir</u>: Same exercise as the preceding one:

<u>Examples</u>:

J'ai su lire à cinq ans. (= *mastered* reading at five)

Je *savais* lire à cinq ans. (= <u>by</u> *the age of 5, I already knew* how to read)

Je *savais* qu'elle allait partir. (= *I knew all along*)

J'ai su qu'elle allait partir. (= *I learned, I found out*)

1. Je _____ déjà nager quand on m'a donné ma première leçon de natation.

2. Je _____ nager sitôt après avoir perdu ma peur irrationnelle de l'eau.

3. Si nous _____ qu'il allait neiger, nous serions restés bien au chaud à la maison !

4. _____-vous où se trouve le bureau de poste ? (two possibilities)

5. Si je _____ qu'il ferait si chaud et humide, je ne serais pas venu.

6. Il faut absolument qu'il _____ son rôle par cœur avant la répétiton.

5. Synthèse : Translate the following sentences.

<u>Examples</u>:

*Tu ne **devrais** pas essayer de le faire, si tu ne <u>le</u> **peux** pas.*

You **should** not try to do it, if you **can't**.

1. You should not have done it.

2. You must have seen him today.

3. I tried several times and finally I was able to do it.

4. I kept trying, but I couldn't do it. (two solutions)

5. They are to visit us next week.

6. I cannot walk, I twisted my ankle.

7. I can sing, but I cannot sing so high!

8. I could not have said it better.

9. The prisoner tried to escape, but he could not reach the fence.

Chapter 11

The active, passive and pronominal voices

Les voix active, passive et pronominale

A grammatical *voice* can be defined as the articulation between a *verb* and its grammatical *subject*. There are three voices in French and English: The active, the passive and the pronominal (or middle) voices.

1) In the *active* voice, the focus is placed on a *subject*, which performs directly the action. The subject (or theme) in the following examples is the *company*:

Examples:

La compagnie a terminé *le projet comme prévu.*

The company has completed *the project as planned.*

2) In the *passive* voice, the focus is reversed: the *object* of the action becomes the subject of the verb: the theme is now the *project*, and the company is now called the *agent* of the process:

Examples:

The project has been completed **by the company** *as planned.*

Le projet a été terminé **par la compagnie** *comme prévu.*

3) In the ***pronominal*** voice, the action is presented as if working on its own power, in a boomerang-like process! An object pronoun refers back to the subject, <u>without the need of an outside agent</u>. It is called *pronominal* because it uses a pronoun to complete the action:

Examples:

*The project **achieved itself** (= ended) as planned.*

*Le projet **s'est terminé** comme prévu.*

The object pronoun, ***s'***, reflects the subject, <u>the projet</u>, like a mirror. And the *company* is now left out of the picture completely.

I. The active voice:

Up until now, most of the examples cited from the beginning of this book had been in the ***active*** voice. It is by far the voice most often used in French, since the French mind generally tends to view an action from the perspective of its cause (i.e., the subject). When English states in the passive voice: ***He was awarded*** a prize, the French sentence would idiomatically be in the active voice: ***On lui a décerné un prix***. This is also due, in this particular case, to the fact that in French the <u>indirect</u> object of a verb (e.g., the prize was awarded ***<u>to him</u>***) <u>cannot</u> be the subject of its corresponding passive verb. This active voice construction is used perhaps, in some situations, to avoid confusion or bizarreness (at least in the French mind!), as a person is not a "thing" being given away or transmitted (e.g., He was awarded, as if it meant he was given away as a gift!).

II. The passive voice:

Though less frequent in French, the passive voice is nevertheless used, but <u>mostly when the agent is expressed</u> in the sentence, introduced by the preposition ***par*** (and less often ***de***):

Examples:

On lui a décerné un prix.

But: *Un prix lui **a été** décerné **par l'association**.*

The system of verb tenses as was presented earlier (e.g., perspectives and aspects) functions exactly as it does in the active voice. In the passive voice, the tense is systematically determined by the added auxiliary verb *être* in the various conjugations:

Examples:

*Le juge **l'avait** condamné à trois mois de prison.*

*Il **avait été** condamné par le juge à trois mois de prison.*

As previously stated, the agent of a passive verb is most often introduced by the preposition ***par*** (= *by*). It is the case when the verb expresses a dynamic action. However, when the verb presents a state of things rather than an action, the preposition ***de*** is often used:

Examples:

*Cette ville **a été** entourée **par** l'ennemi.* (dynamic)

*Cette ville **était** entourée **d'**un solide rempart.* (static)

Note: The preposition *de* is used in so many cases, with so many meanings, that it appears to have eroded most of its original Latin dynamic force. We have seen some cases, and will have more opportunities to witness this again later.

Verbs like ***aimer, respecter, admirer, détester***, etc., that express a state of mind, will usually be followed by ***de*** in the passive voice:

Example:

*Cette enseignante est **respectée de** ses élèves.*

This teacher is **respected by** her students.

When a dynamic situation occurs (e.g., the beginning of respect as an event), the preposition ***par*** returns:

Example:

*Cette enseignante **a été** **respectée** par ses élèves, quand elle **a pris** la défense de l'un d'eux contre l'administration.*

*This teacher **earned the respect of** her students when she sided with one of them against the administration.*

III. The pronominal voice:

Before reviewing the *pronominal voi*ce (which is also used in English, but to a lesser extent), we need to consider two pertinent notions: The **transitive** and **intransitive** nature of verbs (*transit = pass over, transfer, transmit*).

A verb, as the main dynamic part of a sentence, expresses an action or a resulting state. It is said to be **transitive** if it requires an object to complete its meaning.

Example:

*J'ai acheté une **voiture**.*

(The direct object *voiture* brings completion to the action.)

On the other hand, a verb is said to be **intransitive** if it expresses alone the whole action, needing no object to complete its meaning. In fact, it cannot even take an object.

Examples:

*J'arriverai **à cinq heures**.*

*J'arriverai **quand j'arriverai** !*

*J'arriverai **en voiture**.*

Since one cannot "*arriver something*," the three complements above are not objects of the verb, but are called *compléments circonstanciels* (i.e., adverbial phrases). Unlike the objects of the verb, they are not essential to complete the action, but simply provide an <u>additional</u>, often optional, element of either time, place, manner, purpose, etc.

In English and in French, however, many verbs can potentially be *either transitive or intransitive*, depending on the situation.

<u>Examples</u>:

*Avez-vous faim ? --Non, j'ai déjà **mangé**.* (intransitive situation)

*Qu'avez-vous mangé ?-- J'ai mangé **du poisson**.* (transitive situation: *poisson* is the direct object)

*Je **suis** sorti du garage.* (intransitive situation: *garage* is not a direct object, but a circumstantial complement of place)

*I **came** (went) out of the garage.*

*J'**ai** sorti <u>la voiture</u> du garage.* (transitive situation: *voiture* is the direct object; note also the auxiliary verb ***avoir*** with the transitive verb, while *être* is used when it is intransitive)

*I **drove** <u>the car</u> out of the garage.*

Now let us return to the ***pronominal voice***. As indicated in the first page of this chapter, the *pronominal voice* presents a circular, boomerang-like action, whereby the subject and object are one and the same. This is achieved with a personal object pronoun (***me, te, se, nous, vous, se***).

<u>Compare</u>:

*J'ai lavé **ma chemise**.* (active voice)

*Je **me** suis lavé.* (pronominal voice)

*Je **me** suis lavé **les mains**.* (pronominal voice despite the added object, which is an intrinsic part of the person, ***me***, and not viewed as a thing.)

Note: As we have discussed earlier (Chapter 1, #4), a similar process exists in English. Is there a difference between: ***I kicked his leg*** and ***I kicked him in the leg***? In many cases though, and unlike French, the English language seems to treat these situations the same way:

*I washed **my shirt**.* (active voice)

I washed (myself). (pronominal voice: optional pronoun)

*I washed **my hands**.* (active voice)

Whether garment (and other objects) or part of the body, these situations receive the same linguistic treatment in English).

In contrast with English, the French personal pronoun of a pronominal verb <u>must be expressed</u>. When a French verb is in the pronominal voice, the auxiliary verb will always be a form of ***être***. This is logical, if we consider the <u>resulting state</u> of that action.

<u>Examples</u>:

*Je **me** suis réveillé tôt ce matin.* (I can still **<u>be</u>** in a state of ***being*** *réveillé*)

*J'ai **acheté** une voiture.* (I **have** the car, and it is still *achetée*)

IV. <u>Pronominal verbs can express several types of actions</u>:

1) A ***reflexive*** action, whereby the circularity is most evident, as shown in one of the previous examples.

<u>Examples</u>:

*Je **me** suis réveillé tôt ce matin.* (*Je* and *me* are the same person.)

Nous nous *sommes réveillés tôt ce matin.*

(The subjects and objects are the same, each waking up on his own.)

2) A *reciprocal* action, always in the plural, whereby the action is exchanged between at least two components of the subject. The action is mutual, headed in both directions.

Examples:

*Ces deux politiciens **se détestent**.* (each other)

*Ces deux autres **se respectent**.* (each other)

3) An **essentially pronominal** action, with some verbs (about a hundred such French verbs in all), that always use an object pronoun and can never be used in the active or passive voice.

Examples:

*Il **s'est suicidé**.* (self-inflicted by definition.)

He committed suicide.

*Je **m'abstiens** de fumer.* (*abstenir* does not exist without a pronoun.)

I abstain from smoking.

We strive to succeed. *Nous **nous efforçons** de réussir.* (*efforcer* needs a pronoun.)

The bird flew off. *L'oiseau **s'est envolé**.* (*envoler* needs its pronoun.)

4) A pronominal verb with ***a passive meaning and function***:

Examples:

*On peut **lire** ce roman en quelques heures.* (active voice)

*Ce roman peut **être lu** en quelques heures.* (passive voice)

*Ce roman peut **se lire** en quelques heures.* (pronominal voice with a passive meaning: the novel does not literally read itself, but is read.)

Other examples:

*Le français **se parle** en Afrique.* (is spoken)

*Le champagne **se sert** très froid.* (is served)

*Ses livres **se sont vendus** comme des petits pains !* (were sold [or simply sold] like hot cakes)

5) As a general rule, it can be said that **any transitive verb has the potential of becoming a pronominal verb**, given the situation. If indeed the verb can take an object, this object can refer back to the subject. This alone accounts for the vast number of pronominal verbs that appear in French texts.

Example:

On vend *les œufs à la douzaine.*

*Les œufs **se vendent** à la douzaine.*

*Eggs **sell** by the dozen.* (unlike French, the reflexive pronoun is not always expressed in English)

The dynamic and habitual action above must not be confused with a state of things, such as:

*Les œufs sont tous **vendus.***

*Eggs are **sold (out)**.*

In this sentence, the verb is not in the passive voice, since it describes a state of things resulting from an action: The verb is *être* in the present tense and *sold out/vendus* is a mere adjective modifying *les œufs*. This type of word, in this form and function (a past participle), is called **adjectif verbal** (verbal adjective).

Another set of examples will drive the point home:

1) **Action:**

*D'habitude **on sert** le dîner à 7 heures.*

*D'habitude le dîner **se sert** à 7 heures.*

*Dinner **is** customarilly **served** at 7 PM.*

2) **State of things**:

*A table ! le dîner **est servi**.* (= *resting* on the table)

*Come to the table, dinner **is served**.* (= *is here* on the table)

Compare:

*Je suis **levé** depuis 5 heures.* (state - verbal adjective)

*I **have been up** since five.*

*Je **me suis levé** à 5 heures.* (action - reflexive verb)

*I **got up** at five.*

The following paragraph will serve as a recapitulation of the various voices presented in this chapter:

*Ce petit roman **a été écrit** (passive) en quelques semaines. C'est Balzac qui **l'a composé** (active). Il peut **se lire** (passive pronominal) aisément; je **l'ai lu** (active) en trois heures seulement. Mais il est difficile à trouver, car la dernière édition est presque toute **vendue** (verbal adjective). **Dépêchez-vous** (essentially pronominal) d'aller en acheter un exemplaire.*

One last consideration about an action and its after effect:

The auxiliary verb **être** lends itself perfectly to express either an action or its resulting state, depending on the situation.

Examples:

*A quelle heure est-ce que Monsieur Duval **est sorti** ?* (past action: went out)

*Est-ce que Monsieur Duval **est** là ? -- Non, il **est sorti**.* (present resulting state: *he is out*. True he went out earlier at a certain time, but that is not the issue; *he is out now*).

EXERCISES

1. Voix passive vs. verbal adjective: Translate the following sentences, identifying the grammatical situation: (VA) = verbal adjective; (PV) = passive voice. (Several contexts are possible).

Examples:

*L'appartement **est loué** depuis hier.* (VA) (= a present state: verbal adjective)

*L'appartement **a été loué** hier.* (PV) (a past action: passive voice)

1. This poster is stuck on the wall. ( )

2. The campaign was rapidly organized. ( )

3. After six long weeks, the work was finally finished. ( )

4. The riot was provoked by a terrorist group. ( )

5. I was exhausted from too much work. ( )

6. We were frightened by a passing tornado. ( )

7. She was thrilled to have won the election. ( )

8. She was thrilled by the result of the election. ( )

2. Transpose the passive voice sentences of the preceding exercise to the active voice. (Not all sentences are in the passive voice).

Example:

*L'appartement **a été loué** hier.* --> ***On a loué** l'appartement hier.*

3. Depending on each case and possibility, transpose the following sentences into one other voice:

Examples:

***On sert** l'apéritif avant le repas.* (active voice)

*L'apéritif **se sert** avant le repas.* (pronominal voice)

*L'apéritif **est servi d'habitude** avant le repas.* (passive voice)

1. On parle français dans une bonne partie de l'Afrique.

2. Le bridge est joué à quatre.

3. Cette règle de grammaire est comprise par tout le monde.

4. On doit boire le champagne très froid.

5. Cette coutume ne s'observe nulle part ailleurs.

6. On n'avait encore jamais vu cela.

7. Cela ne se fait pas dans la bonne société !

8. Elle est bien appréciée par son employeur.

9. On n'aurait jamais vu un tel manque de tact autrefois.

10. « On gouverne mieux les hommes par leurs vices que par leurs vertus. » (Napoléon)

3. Translate the following sentences.

1. He was seen to enter the house.

2. He was seen to enter the house by a few witnesses.

3. If I did that, I would be laughed at.

4. If I proposed that, my opinion wouldn't be listened to.

5. The doctor was sent for.

6. In the long run everything is known.

7. Albert Camus got killed in a car accident.

8. Why do people kill one another instead of helping each others?

9. One must mistrust at times the motivations of certain persons.

4. Rewrite the following text using verbs in the active or pronominal voices, whenever the grammatical situation allows it. *(As a bonus, this is an authentic recipe!)*

Comment le pain est fait par un boulanger

Cinq tasses de farine sont versées dans un grand bol, à quoi sont ajoutées une cuillérée à soupe de sel fin et une demi-cuillérée à café de levure en poudre. Le tout est ensuite bien mélangé. Puis deux tasses et demie d'eau froide ou tiède sont ajoutées, ainsi qu'une cuillérée à soupe d'huile d'olive. Ensuite tous ces ingrédients sont bien mélangés pour former une pâte souple et homogène, ni trop liquide, ni trop sèche.

Le bol est alors couvert d'une pellicule plastique et mis de côté pour laisser fermenter et lever la pâte pendant au moins dix heures. Lorsque la pâte a doublé de volume, elle est versée et roulée sur une surface couverte d'un peu de farine, avant qu'elle soit remise dans un grand bol huilé (pour éviter qu'elle colle). Puis la pâte est laissée à lever encore une fois pendant au moins une heure. La pâte est alors prête à être métamorphosée en pain !

Le four est alors chauffé à 400 degrés Fahrenheit, avec à l'intérieur une grande marmite métallique vide surmontée de son couvercle (des ustensiles conçus tous les deux pour aller au four).

Lorsque la température du four est montée à 400 degrés, la pâte est alors versée dans la marmite brûlante et le couvercle est aussitôt remis en place sur la marmite. Au bout d'une heure de cuisson, le couvercle est enlevé pour laisser dorer le pain pendant un quart d'heure de plus. La marmite est alors retirée du four et le pain, qui se détache bien, est mis à refroidir sur une planche à découper en bois.

Bon appétit !

Jacques Bourgeacq

Chapter 12

The infinitive mood

Le mode infinitif

For this chapter, we have chosen a comparative approach, as it seemed to be a more productive way of presenting the complexity of the infinitive mood, a complexity of usage that hides behind its simplicity of form.

In both languages, the infinitive presents a verb (action or state) in its purely conceptual meaning, without any indication of person (*je, tu,* etc.), number (singular/plural), and conjugations. It is "verb in the raw." This general status gives the infinitive, as we shall see, great flexibility. This is especially true since, while being a verb, it can also assume all the functions of a noun. This versatility of functions explains the frequent use of the infinitive.

As a verb, since it does not compete with the gerund (as is the case in English), the French infinitive is used all the more frequently.

Examples:

*I want **to speak** with you.* (infinitive)

*I like **speaking** with you.* (gerund)

*I like **to swim**/ I like **swimming*** (both gerund and infinitive)

*I enjoy **swimming**.* (gerund)

In French, when a verb is the <u>object</u> of another verb, <u>the second will be in the infinitive mood</u>. In English, on the other hand, the choice of infinitive or gerund is *the* challenging part, often determined by each leading verb. French, on the other hand, <u>always</u> requires the infinitive when it is the object of a leading verb. But, as we shall see, the real challenge is in <u>the choice of a connecting preposition</u> (which one?) or no preposition at all, depending on the <u>regimen</u> (rule) of each individual leading verb.

<u>Examples:</u>

*J'aime **nager**.* (infinitive) - *I enjoy **swimming**.* (gerund)

*La loi **interdit <u>de</u> fumer** dans les lieux publics.* - *The law **forbids smoking** in public places.*

*J'aime **jouer** au tennis.* (no connecting preposition) - *I like **playing** tennis.*

I. The infinitive as subject of a verb:

As subject of a verb, the infinitive functions as a noun:

***Vouloir**, c'est pouvoir.*

***Travailler** est nécessaire pour réussir.*

***Partir**, c'est **mourir** un peu.*

II. The infinitive as object of a verb:

There is a vast number of verbs that can have an infinitive as object, each requiring a specific preposition (*à* or *de*) or none at all, before the infinitive:

Examples:

*Nous désirons **acheter** cette voiture.*

*Nous refusons **d'acheter** cette voiture.*

*Nous songeons **à acheter** cette voiture.* (*songer* = to consider)

The whole system appears capricious, and to a great extent it is. Linguistic research has not found an overall logic that would permit a foolproof rational choice of prepositions. So far, sheer memorization has been the solution.

Some suggestions, however, can help:

There are certain principles or cues that may at least help reduce our reliance on pure memory.

Once again, we shall resort to Latin grammar, which may provide partial and hypothetical solutions. The French prepositions *à* and *de* are directly derived from Latin, with similar meanings:

Latin ***ad*** = *to, toward, near to,* and *for.*

Latin ***de*** = *from, down from, concerning,* and *about.*

Latin had another preposition, ***ab*** (= *from*). Over time, ***ad*** (*to*) and ***ab*** (*from*) eroded into one single French preposition: *à*, which can have either meaning, depending on the situation at hand:

Examples:

Donner quelque chose à quelqu'un (***ad*** --> give to)

Voler quelque chose à quelqu'un (***ab*** --> steal from)

*Je **lui** ai acheté sa voiture.* (***lui*** = *à* Pierre = ***from*** Pierre)

*Le voyou **m'**a enlevé mon portefeuille.* (= lifted ***from*** me)

So, aside from memorizing long lists of verbs and their prepositions, it may be helpful to submit each leading verb to a test: the idea of movement, either *to* or *from* the infinitive:

Examples:

Je commence à avoir peur. (moving toward *peur*)

Je refuse de partir. (moving away from the idea of *partir*)

J'ai un devoir à faire. (moving toward the homework)

Arrête de faire ce bruit ! (pushing away from the noise)

Note: This hypothetical approach will not always work, as there may be of course other unknown factors involved, including a share of arbitrariness.

There are also other cues for selecting the proper construction:

1) A number of constructions with ***avoir* + *noun* + *infinitive***

use ***de***:

J'ai besoin de prendre des vacances.

Qui a envie d'aller au cinéma ?

Qui n'a pas peur de mourir ?

Logically, such infinitives modify a noun in a type relation (eg., the type of fear is from death): --> ***de*** (cf. Chapter 3, The complements of nouns).

2) Declarative verbs, such as ***déclarer, dire, demander, prier, suggérer, ordonner***, etc., connect with the infinitive using ***de***.

Examples:

On m'a demandé de signer ce document.

Je vous prie de répondre à ma question.

Elle m'a suggéré de ne rien dire.

III. The infinitive as object of an adjective:

Etre + adjective + infinitive --> de:

Examples:

Je suis enchanté de faire votre connaissance.

Est-ce qu'on est obligé de suivre ce cours ?

As explained in Chapter 4 (last section), there are two possible constructions with **être, sembler, paraître**:

1) With impersonal expressions: *Il est + adjective* --> **de**:

Il est facile de faire cette erreur.

Il semble facile de faire cette erreur.

2) With straight (i.e. not impersonal) constructions --> **à**:

Voilà une erreur facile à faire. (erreur = object of *faire*; and

movement toward error)

Cette erreur paraît facile à faire. (movement toward the error)

IV. The infinitive in adverbial phrases:

Unlike English prepositions, that can introduce a gerund, a French verb preceded by any preposition will be in the infinitive mood:

Examples:

*They left **without saying** goodbye.*

*Ils sont partis **sans** **dire** au revoir.*

*I got up right **after** **waking up**.*

*Je me suis levé sitôt **après m'être réveillé**.*

Note: One exception is the preposition **en** + gerund, which will be discussed in the next chapter.

V. The infinitive replacing a conjugated verb or a whole clause:

The syntax can often be changed, as the infinitive can form a tight unit with the main verb. This is another case of synthetic vs analytic phrasing, as presented in the chapter on the qualifying adjectives (Value # 3: Chapter 5,2, The French synthetic view).

Examples:

*Je **voyais** l'autobus **qui arrivait**.* (analytic unit)

*Je **voyais arriver** l'autobus.* (synthetic unit)

*J'**entendais** les enfants **qui criaient**.*

*J'**entendais crie**r les enfants.*

*Il jurait **qu'il avait dit** la vérité.*

*Il jurait **avoir dit** la vérité.*

Note: It seems as if the two separate actions, *voir* and *arriver*, were combined into one single mental operation of the beholder.

VI. The infinitive replacing the imperative mood:

In administrative style, commands or directions are written in the infinitive, rather than in the imperative mood as in English. The imperative personalizes, as it addresses the reader here and now in the second person (you), while the infinitive is valid for just any time and anybody, thus softening the command with a generalization. The infinitive seems to be the direct object of an understood (unexpressed) main verb: *Il faut, On doit, Il est important de...*

Examples:

Ne pas se pencher au-dehors. (not *Ne vous penchez pas*) (At the window of a train)

*Complét**er** les phrases suivantes...* (not *Complét**ez***)

En cas d'urgence, *s'adress**er** à...* (not *Adress**ez-vous***)

*Ralent**ir**, école.* (not *Ralentiss**ez***)

Alternate infinitive constructions replacing the imperative:

*Prière de ne pas fumer/ **Défense de fumer*** - *Do not* **smoke**/ *No smoking*

Stationnement **interdit** - *No parking*

VII. The passive infinitive:

The infinitive can be used in the passive voice:

Example:

*En conduisant trop vite, on risque d'**être arrêté** par la police.* - Driving too fast, one risks **being arrested** by the police.

There is a short series of verbs, however, that take an infinitive in the active voice, though the idea is passive: *entendre, s'entendre, voir, se voir, se laisser, faire, se faire.* (Note also that the English construction uses a past participle, not an infinitive).

Examples:

*En conduisant trop vite, on risque de **se faire arrêter** par la police.* -

*Driving too fast, one risks **getting arrest<u>ed</u>** by the police.*

*Elle ne <u>se laisse</u> pas **march<u>er</u>** sur les pieds. - She does not <u>let herself be stepp<u>ed</u> on</u>.*

VIII. <u>The past infinitive</u>:

When the action of the infinitive <u>precedes</u> the leading verb in time, a past infinitive is used. It is the closest thing to a verb tense for the infinitive. English may or may not stress this time lapse between the two actions:

<u>Examples</u>:

*I got up right after **waking up**.*

*I got up right after **having awakened**.*

In contrast, French will stress this time relation more frequently:

<u>Examples</u>:

*Il est parti sans **laisser** d'adresse.* (possible simultaneous actions)

*Il est parti sans **avoir laissé** d'adresse.* (*laisser* prior to *partir*)

*On n'entre pas au cinéma avant **d'avoir présenté** son ticket.* (showing first the ticket)

IX. <u>Some infinitives have become full-fledged nouns</u>:

In medieval French, the infinitive was frequently used as a noun, with or without an article. A number of these cases resisted the erosion of time, probably due to their very frequent use:

<u>Examples</u>:

le déjeuner, le dîner, le souper

le rire, un sourire

un lever/un coucher de soleil (a sunrise/a sunset)

un aller et retour (a round trip)

le savoir-faire (the know-how)

le laissez-faire

le bon vouloir (good will)

un être humain (a human being)

le devoir (duty, homework)

un pourboire (a tip)

Prendre le pouvoir

Au revoir !

EXERCISES

1. Complete this text with <u>infinitives</u> and connecting prepositions as needed. (Remember that an English gerund is not necessarily a gerund in French!)

This excerpt is from Guy de Maupassant's short story "Toine," a café owner, known for his verve and peculiar hospitality...

Ah! oui, on le connaissait Toine Brûlot, le plus gros homme du canton, et même de l'arrondissement. Sa petite maison semblait dérisoirement trop étroite et trop basse (to contain him) _____, et quand on le voyait debout sur sa porte où il passait des journées entières, on se demandait comment il (could enter) _____ dans sa demeure. Il y entrait chaque fois que se présentait un consommateur, car Toine-ma-Fine était invité de droit (to levy) _____ son petit verre sur tout ce que (one drank) _____ chez lui.

Son café avait pour enseigne : « Au Rendez-vous des Amis », et il était bien, le *pé* Toine, l'ami de toute la contrée. On venait de Fécamp, et de Montivilliers (to see him) _____ et (to have a laugh) _____ en l'écoutant, comme il (would have made laugh) _____ une pierre de tombe, ce gros homme. Il avait une manière (of kidding) _____ les gens sans (angering them) _____, (of winking) _____ de l'œil (to express) _____ ce qu'il ne disait pas, (of tapping himself) _____ sur la cuisse dans ses accès de gaieté qui vous tirait le rire du ventre malgré vous, à tous les coups. Et puis c'était une curiosité rien que de (watching him drink) _____. Il buvait tant qu'on lui en offrait, et de tout, avec une joie dans son œil malin, une joie qui venait de son double plaisir, plaisir de (treating himself) _____ d'abord et (cashing in) _____ des gros sous, ensuite, pour sa régalade. (Guy de Maupassant, "Toine," 1885)

2. Simplify the sentences below with an infinitive construction (In contrast with the English gerund). Remember that the syntax will often be modified by the change.

Example:

*Nous le regardions **qui découpait** ses cartons.*

*Nous le regardions **découper** ses cartons.*

1. Il prétend qu'il a fait tout ce chemin à pied.

2. Nous vîmes une longue file de voitures qui arrivait.

3. J'ai souvent entendu qu'on le disait.

4. La prison était pleine de rats : je les sentais qui me couraient sur le corps.

5. Nous regardions le niveau de l'eau qui montait.

6. Il affirme qu'il sait piloter un avion.

7. Je crois que je peux le faire aisément.

8. Ayant payé toutes ses dettes, il était content qu'il ne devait plus rien à personne.

9. Pensez-vous que vous pourrez nous mener à l'aéroport ?

10. Et j'entends le train qui siffle dans le soir.

3. Impersonal vs. personal expression: Il est + adjective vs. adjective with personal verb.

Examples:

*Il est utile <u>de</u> savoir les règles, mais elles ne sont pas toujours **faciles** <u>à</u> appliquer.*

Impersonal phrase --> *de*

adjective + movement *toward* --> *à*

1. Ce que tu proposes est plus facile _____ dire que _____ faire.

2. Il est toujours plus facile _____ critiquer que _____ créer.

3. Il nous semble impossible _____ achever à temps notre projet.

4. Voilà une formule impossible _____ appliquer.

5. Il est important _____ savoir au préalable l'opinion du public.

6. Oui en effet, ce facteur est très important _____ établir.

7. Ce nouveau restaurant reçoit de bonnes critiques. C'est bon _____ savoir !

8. Il est toujours utile _____ regarder le menu à la porte du restaurant avant d'entrer.

4. Is it _à_, _de_ or no preposition? Complete the following infinitive constructions.

Examples:

*On nous **oblige à** travailler le week-end.* (movement **toward** --> **à**)

*Je ne suis pas **content de** travailler le week-end.* (adjective + infinitive --> **de**)

1. En fait, tu me reproches _____ avoir essayé _____ t'aider.

2. Je vous suggère _____ le forcer _____ vous donner une réponse ferme.

3. Je crois _____ avoir assez insisté là-dessus, et je regrette _____ avoir _____ vous le rappeler.

4. On m'a défendu _____ en parler; j'hésite donc _____ soulever la question.

5. Je me félicite _____ vous voir tous réunis ici.

6. Je considère _____ avoir assez travaillé dans ma vie. Après tout, il ne me reste que peu d'années _____ vivre. D'ailleurs je rêve _____ passer mon temps _____ voyager.

7. J'ai du mal _____ m'habituer _____ manger tous les jours au restaurant.

8. Evitez _____ soulever ce sujet en sa présence.

9. Contentez-vous _____ répondre à la question.

10. Accepteriez-vous _____ prendre la direction du projet ?

11. Je vous remercie _____ avoir répondu si promptement à mon courriel.

12. Faites attention _____ ne pas le vexer. Je vous recommande _____ être très diplomate avec lui. Sinon vous risqueriez _____ le perdre.

13. Je m'attends _____ recevoir de ses nouvelles prochainement.

14. Je suis obligé _____ changer de vol, le mien a été annulé.

15. J'ai un travail énorme _____ terminer avant la fin de la semaine.

16. Après le crash bancaire, nous en sommes réduits _____ vivre d'une toute petite pension.

17. Nous estimons _____ vous avoir laissé assez de temps pour vous préparer.

18. Alors ça sert à quoi _____ faire des études ? --Ça sert _____ ne pas trouver d'emploi quand on a obtenu son diplôme !

19. Je ne souhaite à personne _____ passer par les mêmes ennuis que moi.

20. Pardonnez-moi _____ vous interrompre, mais sans vouloir _____ vous presser _____ conclure, nous avons bien dépassé l'heure _____ libérer la salle !

5. Passive or active infinitives? Translate the following sentences:

Examples:

*Je ne l'ai jamais vu **faire**.* (passive idea, active form)

*I have never seen it **done**.* (passive voice)

1. Don't let yourself be influenced.

2. He got himself killed.

3. I have never heard it explained.

4. I saw the child being kidnapped.

5. They had their travel expenses paid.

6. Don't let yourself be pushed around! (use a form of *faire*)

7. He got fired from his job.

8. He got caught red handed.

6. Soften the command with an alternate infinitive construction:

Example:

Ne descendez pas tu train en marche.

--> ***Ne pas descendre*** *du train en marche.*

--> ***Défense de descendre*** *du train en marche*

(**Do not get off** the train while in motion.)

1. Hôpital ! Ne klaxonnez pas.

2. (On a highway) Ne doublez pas.

3. (On a street) Ne stationnez pas.

4. Ne jetez pas d'ordures.

5. Rue piétonne, ne circulez pas en voiture.

6. Passage privé : n'entrez pas.

7. N'affichez pas (sur ce mur).

8. (At the zoo) Ne donnez pas à manger aux animaux.

Chapter 13

The present participle and the gerund

Le participe présent et le gérondif

I. <u>The present participle</u>:

The word <u>participle</u> (*participe*) refers to the idea of ***part**aking* in the action of another verb. There are two verbal forms that come under that name: *present participle* and *past participle*. And both have the dynamic force of verbs, in their own way and degree.

We encountered the *past participle* during our discussion on the indicative mood tenses: *passé composé, plus-que-parfait*, etc. (cf. Chapter 7).

The *present participle* is the other verbal form, expressing an <u>action parallel with, and separate from, a leading (main) verb</u>. (Why *present*? The term is simply to distinguish it from the *past* participle, used in compound past tenses). Unlike the past participle, the *present participle* is <u>invariable</u> in form (no gender, no number). It often replaces a subordinate clause or a conjugated verb.

<u>Example</u>:

*J'ai vu des soldats **qui défilaient** dans la rue.*

*J'ai vu des soldats **défil<u>ant</u>** dans la rue.*

*(I saw soldiers **marching (who marched)** in the street.)*

(Another construction: cf. preceding chapter, section V)

*J'**ai vu défiler** des **soldats** dans la rue.* (**ai vu défiler** = *a tight, subjective unit connected to the subject **je**; **soldats** can be analyzed as object of **ai vu défiler**)*

The present participle tends to express an <u>action</u>, while the past participle often presents a <u>state of things</u>. In fact, the past participle is often used as a verbal adjective, while the present participle tends to remain a dynamic verb.

<u>Examples:</u>

*Il regardait la rue, **penché** à la fenêtre.* (a state)

*Il regardait la rue, **se penchant** à la fenêtre.* (an action)

*(He was watching the street, **leaning** at the window.)*

In the first French sentence above, the verb in its past participle form (*penché*) is <u>static</u>, frozen almost like a snapshot. Thus ***penché*** is like an adjective. By contrast, the second sentence stresses the <u>dynamism</u> of the action (*se penchant*), expressing movement, almost like in a video.

A number of verbs in the present participle, however, have become "frozen" into full-fledged nouns. (This happened also with past participles: e.g. *un réfugié, un blessé, une employée*).

<u>Examples:</u>

commercer --> commerçant --> un commerçant (a merchant)

tenir lieu (de) -->tenant lieu --> un lieutenant (a lieutenant)

tourner --> tournant --> un tournant (a curve in the road)

restaurer --> restaurant --> un restaurant (a restaurant)

*fabri**qu**er* --> *fabri**qu**ant* --> *un fabri**c**ant* (a manufacturer)

This last example shows a spelling difference that has occurred between many present participles as verbs and the nouns derived from them. To form a present participle, the infinitive suffix (*-er/ir/re*, etc.) is replaced by the suffix *-ant*. Thus *fabriquer* gives *fabriquant*. Over time, however, the spelling of the corresponding nouns or adjectives was simplified for such words as *fabri**c**ant* (*c* instead of *qu*), probably to tell apart verb from noun or adjective...

Other notable examples of these spelling changes: *convainquant, fatiguant, naviguant, communiquant, intriguant, excellant*, etc.

Examples:

*Voilà un discours **convainquant** le public.* (verb: *which convinces the public*)

*Voilà un discours **convaincant**.* (adjective: *convincing, persuasive*)

*C'est un médecin **excellant** dans sa profession.* (verb: *who excels*)

*C'est un médecin **excellent**.* (adjective)

*Cette méthode, **différant** de la précédente, est plus productive.* (verb: *which differs*)

*C'est une méthode **différente**.* (adjective)

When used as a noun or an adjective, the present participle varies in gender and number.

Examples:

*Ces gens sont des **intrigants**.*

*Une histoire **amusante**.*

*Des dépenses **extravagantes**.*

II. The gerund:

The French gerund (*le gérondif*) has a more limited use than the English gerund, which apparently includes <u>most verb forms ending in -*ing*</u>.

The French gerund, by contrast, modifies the leading verb <u>only as an adverbial complement</u>, as it provides a circumstance (simultaneity or manner) of the action expressed by that leading verb. It is usually preceded by the preposition *en* (*while, by*).

Examples:

*Nous marchions **en chantant**.*

(adverbial phrase: two simultaneous actions, one modifying the other, with *en* = *while*; the gerund indicates here <u>how</u> we walked)

*C'est **en étudiant** qu'on réussit à ses examens.*

(adverbial phrase: two consecutive actions, one <u>causing</u> the other; *en* = *by, in so doing*)

More examples:

*Le bébé s'est endormi **en pleurant**.*

(either *while* or *by*; although "The baby cried himself to sleep" indicates more clearly the cause and effect relation)

*C'est **en forgeant** qu'on devient forgeron.* (***en*** = *by, by dint of*)

By smithing one becomes a smith.

(But, more idiomatically, this is a proverb corresponding to "Practice makes perfect").

The action of the gerund can be stressed by adding the adverb **tout**, often expressing a <u>contradiction</u> or an <u>opposition</u>.

Examples:

*Il mène une vie de débauche **tout en prêchant** la morale.*

He leads a life of debauchery **all the while** preaching morality.

*Elle s'en va, **bien qu'elle sache** que cela me rend triste.* (though she knows)

*Elle s'en va, **tout en sachant** que cela me rend triste.* (though knowing full well)

Another limitation of the French gerund:

The gerund continues the action of the subject of the main verb.

Examples:

*Il a vu sa cousine **dansant** avec un bel officier.* (present participle)

*Il a vu sa cousine **en dansant** avec un bel officier.* (gerund)

Who was dancing with whom? He or his cousin? The **gerund + en** relates to the subject, *il*, while the present participle relates to the closer word, **cousine** (*cousine dansant = cousine qui dansait*).

Gerund or infinitive?

Due to the many uses of the English gerund, Anglophone students of French often hesitate between the gerund and the infinitive forms. The choice depends on the answer to one question: ***How many actions are involved***? One or two? If one action, then use the infinitive; if two actions, use the gerund:

Examples:

*Flaubert a passé six ans **à écrire** Madame Bovary.*

*Flaubert **spent** six years **writing** Madame Bovary.* (*spending* and *writing* are in fact blended into one single action: = *he wrote for 6 years*)

Jacques Bourgeacq

En écrivant <u>Madame Bovary</u>, *Flaubert* **lisait** *des revues de médecine.*

Writing <u>Madame Bovary</u>, Flaubert read medical journals. (<u>two</u> simultaneous and separate actions: *writing* and *reading*).

EXERCISES

I. Complete the following text with gerund, present participle or verbal adjectives, according to the context. Indicate also in each case the type of word: (G) gerund, (PP) present participle, or (VA) verbal adjective:

This is an excerpt from <u>La Nuit de mai</u>, *by the romantic poet Alfred de Musset. He imagines a dialogue with his Muse, who warns him of the role and destiny of any great poet: the pelican's legendary suicide serves as a symbol for a poet's self-sacrifice for his public...*

Les plus désespérés sont les chants les plus beaux,

Et j'en sais d'immortels qui sont de purs sanglots.

Lorsque le pélican, lassé d'un long voyage,

Dans les brouillards du soir retourne à ses roseaux,

Ses petits affamés courent sur le rivage

En (seeing him) _____ au loin s'abattre sur les eaux:

Déjà, (thinking) _____ saisir et partager leur proie,

Ils courent à leur père avec de cris de joie

En (shaking) _____ leur becs sur leur goitres hideux.

Lui, (reaching) _____ à pas lents une roche élevée,

De son aile (hanging) _____ (sheltering) _____ sa couvée,

Côte à Côte 2

Pêcheur mélancolique, il regarde les cieux.

Le sang coule à longs flots de sa poitrine ouverte;

En vain il a des mers fouillé la profondeur:

L'Océan était vide et la plage déserte;

Pour toute nourriture il apporte son coeur.

Sombre et silencieux, (lying, stretched out) _____ sur la pierre,

(Sharing) _____ à ses fils ses entrailles de père,

Dans son amour sublime il berce sa douleur,

Et, (watching) _____ couler sa (bleeding) _____mamelle,

Sur son festin de mort il s'affaisse et chancelle,

Ivre de volupté, de tendresse et d'horreur.

Mais parfois, au milieu du divin sacrifice,

Fatigué de mourir dans un trop long supplice

Il craint que ses enfants ne le laissent (living, alive) _____;

Alors il se soulève, ouvre son aile au vent,

Et, se (striking) _____le coeur avec un cri sauvage,

Il pousse dans la nuit un si funèbre adieu,

Que les oiseaux des mers désertent le rivage,

Et que le voyageur attardé sur la plage,

(Sensing) _____ passer la mort, se recommande à Dieu.

Poète, c'est ainsi que font les grands poètes.

Ils laissent s'égayer ceux qui vivent un temps;

Mais les festins humains qu'ils servent à leurs fêtes

Ressemblent la plupart à ceux des pélicans.

(Alfred de Musset, *La Nuit de mai*, 1835).

2. Gerund or infinitive? Complete the following sentences:

<u>Examples:</u>

*Il s'amuse **à écrire** des poèmes*. (one action: the writing itself is fun)

*Il s'amuse **en écrivant** des poèmes*. (two actions: writing and perhaps teasing the cat for fun!)

1. Ce n'est que (by reading) _____ ce texte plusieurs fois qu'on arrive à le comprendre.

2. Il gagne sa vie (writing) _____ des romans.

3. Flaubert a passé six ans (writing) _____ <u>Madame Bovary</u>.

4. J'aime écouter de la musique (while working) _____.

5. J'ai passé une heure (listening to) _____ ses récriminations.

6. Elle écoutait son histoire (laughing) _____.

7. Ce n'est pas (by watching me) _____ que vous allez apprendre à le faire.

8. Je me tue (repeating) _____ sans cesse la même chose.

9. Il s'est tué (cleaning) _____ son revolver.

10. Elle adore (listening) _____ du Bach.

12. (While claiming) _____ des intentions pacifiques, ce pays est en guerre depuis vingt ans !

3. Gerund or present participle? Complete the following sentences:

Examples:

*Je l'ai vue **qui traversait** la rue.*

*Je l'ai vue **traversant (traverser)** la rue.* (*she* was the one crossing)

*Je l'ai vue **alors que je traversais** la rue.*

*Je l'ai vue **en traversant** la rue.* (*I* was the one crossing)

1. Le client observait la serveuse (débarrasser) _____ la table.

2. Il a laissé tomber un verre (débarrasser) _____ la table.

3. La météo (annoncer) _____ de la pluie, je laisse mon vélo chez moi.

4. On apprend mieux une langue (l'enseigner) _____.

5. Je ne me pressais pas, (être) _____ sûr d'avoir manqué mon train.

6. Il aperçut sa cousine (danser) _____ avec un bel officier. (two solutions; explain them)

4. Present participle or past participle? Translate the following sentences:

Examples:

***En se penchant** à la fenêtre, il est tombé.* - **Leaning** *out of the window, he fell off.* (dynamic situation)

*Il restait des heures **penché** à la fenêtre.* (static situation) - *He spent hours **leaning** out of the window.*

1. She was not dead. She was sleeping.

2. He was sleeping on the sofa, and the TV was on.

3. The clothes were hanging on a line outside. (use *étendre*)

4. The children were quiet, sitting in front of the TV.

5. We found him lying on the floor.

6. Sitting in the waiting room, she picked up a magazine.

7. Standing to attention, he saluted the general.

8. They were there, standing and doing nothing.

5. The gerund replacing an adverbial clause. Transpose the following sentences into a gerund or present participle construction:

Examples:

Elle s'en va, **bien qu'elle sache** *que cela me peine.*

Elle s'en va, **tout en sachant** *que cela me peine.*

1. *Si vous vous y preniez* autrement, cela irait peut-être mieux !

2. *Comme je ne savais pas* où vous habitiez, je suis allé à l'hôtel.

3. La fortune vient *lorsqu'on dort.* (proverb)

4. *Comme je n'avais reçu* aucune réponse, j'ai récrit.

5. *Bien qu'il ait prétendu* m'aider, il a causé mon échec.

6. Il écoute les informations *et mange en même temps.*

7. *Après qu'il eut payé l'addition*, il se leva et sortit.

8. Il a refusé de témoigner, *parce qu'il craignait* pour sa vie.

6. Summing up the gerund, infinitive, present participle, and noun. Translate the following sentences:

Examples:

*J'aime **faire** de la poterie.* - I like **making** pottery.

Marcher/ La marche *est un excellent exercice.* - **Walking** is an excellent exercise.

1. A nurse is accustomed to seeing blood.

2. The whole text needs editing.

3. Quit teasing me!

4. Seeing is believing.

5. She is taking dancing lessons.

6. We did not see the oncoming car.

7. They walked without noticing us.

8. You should not spend all day watching television.

9. By arriving early, finding a place will be easier.

10. You should stop smoking and start exercising instead.

11. I have no intention of quitting my job.

12. We spent our vacation in a fishing village.

13. Swimming is a complete sport.

Jacques Bourgeacq

Chapter 14

Some problematic prepositions

Quelques prépositions problématiques

The role of a *preposition* is to <u>connect</u> two elements of a sentence in a particular relation forming a <u>new unit of meaning</u>.

<u>Example</u>:

*Elle dansait **avec grâce**.* (*avec* introduces *grâce*, indicating the manner of the action *dansait*).

Both English and French possess a vast number of prepositions that express an even greater number of potential relations (*time, place, manner, comparison, purpose, opposition, cause,* etc.). An exhaustive study is not possible here, as it would require a very thick book. We will thus limit this chapter to a few prepositions that have been stumbling blocks for English speakers. This situation usually occurs when one preposition in one language can have several meanings, while it has only one meaning, or other different meanings, in the other language. A classic example is the English preposition *for*, when expressing <u>time</u>. Conveying several distinct situations, it takes three French equivalents to express them: ***pour, depuis***, and ***pendant***. This type of situation requires an explanation and, whenever possible and necessary, the exploration of a different mode of mental representation.

Many prepositions correspond in both English and French,

demanding just an effort of memorization as mere vocabulary. Others, grounded in a different conception, require new thinking, as we shall see.

So far, we have encountered a few prepositions in previous chapters:

1) the prepositions connecting the object of a noun: e.g. *une machine **à** laver, une salle **de** bain* (Chapter 3)

2) the prepositions connecting an infinitive to a leading verb: *apprendre **à** nager, refuser **de** sortir* (Chapter 12)

We will now proceed, in a comparative approach, to a selection of prepositions that have shown to be problematic or confusing for the English-speaker.

I. *FOR* as a preposition of time:

1) **Pour**:

*Il **part** demain **pour** une semaine.* - He **is leaving** tomorrow **for** a week.

(*Pour* is used here to project a duration into the future, from a verb with a *punctual or an initial* aspect: *il part*; cf. Aspects, Chapter 7).

*Il **partait** le lendemain **pour** une semaine.* - He **was leaving** the next day **for** a week.

(Identical situation as in the above sentence, but the action is projected from a past perspective into what was then a future).

2) **Depuis**:

*Elle **habite** ici **depuis** trois ans.* - She **has been living** here **for** three years.

(While English stresses here an action initiated in the past (*has been living*) and suggests continuation in the present, French emphasizes the perspective of the present using a durative aspect (*habite* = is living). It is the preposition **depuis** that points back to the beginning of the action. *For* emphasizes duration. Conclusion? Both languages are right in their vision: reality has many facets!)

*Elle **habitait** ici **depuis** trois ans, quand elle mourut.* - She **had been living** here *for* three years, when she died.

(Identical situation as in the above sentence, but the **whole action** is projected into a more distant past). But the vision of one language cannot be applied to the other language. To each his own!

Note: English speakers are also confused at times between **depuis** and **dès**. **Dès** places the verb at a specific point in time, whether past, present or future:

*Il se lève chaque matin **dès** 7 heures.* (gets up as early as 7 o'clock).

But: *Il est levé **depuis** 7 heures.* (he has been *up since* 7 o'clock.)

3) **Pendant**:

*Elle **a habité** ici **pendant** trois ans.* - She **lived** here *for* three years.

Pendant is used here to project the action totally into the past, detached from the present (unlike case # 2 above). The temporal aspect is global; the 3-year stay may have been decades ago, having nothing to do with the present, which is the point of perspective).

*Elle **avait habité** ici **pendant** trois ans, puis elle a déménagé...* - She **had lived** here *for* three years, and then she moved...

(Identical situation as in the preceding sentence, but projected into a more distant past, and viewed now from a past perspective (i.e. the time when she moved).

4) **Il y a, voilà**:

To complete this temporal system, let's add the peculiar prepositions *il y a* and *voilà* = *ago* (they are actually verb forms turned into prepositions). These prepositions indicate a time void between the perspective and the time of the action. Time has passed between now and the actions, indicating a time vacuum between the two points:

*Elle **a habité** ici **il y a** trois ans.* (*lived*, global aspect)

*Elle **habitait** ici **il y a** trois ans.* (*was living*, durative aspect)

***Voilà** trois ans, elle **habitait** ici.* (same aspect as the preceding example)

(*She **lived** (**was living**) here three years **ago***).

Note: English does not always stress the durative aspect with such forms as ***was living, used to live, would live***; the form ***lived*** often suffices, given the immediate context. And this is precisely the source of confusion in distinguishing between the French *imparfait* and *passé composé* (or *passé simple*), because in this case French forces us to pick only one tense, the right one!

5) **Il y a ... que**:

The prepositional phrase ***Il y a... que*** is not to be confused with plain *il y a*. It is an alternate, emphatic form for ***depuis***:

*Elle **habite** ici **depuis** trois ans.*

***Il y a** trois ans **qu'**elle habite ici.* (No time void: living here has been continuous over 3 years until now, as with *depuis*)

Same situation viewed from a past perspective:

*Elle **habitait** ici **depuis** trois ans, quand elle a quitté la ville.*

***Il y avait** trois ans **qu'**elle habitait ici, quand elle a quitté la ville.*

II. *IN* as a time preposition:

Dans vs. *en*:

The sentence, *I can do the work **in** an hour,* is ambiguous: it may mean: *I can start it an hour from now,* or *I can complete it within an hour* (whenever I start, now, later or at any time).

French distinguishes between these two situations:

*Je peux faire ce travail **dans** une heure.* (= I can start **an hour from now**, with no indication of time length to complete the work)

*Je peux faire ce travail **en** une heure.* (= I can complete the work **within an hour**, *whenever I start*)

III. *IN* as a preposition of manner:

(In connection with the nouns: *manière, façon* --> ***de***)

*Elle joue **d'**une manière habile.* - She plays ***in*** a skillful way.

De *toute façon, je n'en veux pas.* - ***In*** any event, I don't want it.

*Elle me regardait **d'un air amusé**.* - She looked at me ***amusedly***.

<u>With the idea of situation:</u>

*Allez **en** paix.* - Go ***in*** peace.

*Nous travaillons **en** silence.* - We work ***in*** silence.

*La dame **en** blanc.* - The lady ***in*** white.

<u>Note the difference:</u>

*Cet étudiant <u>loge</u> **dans** une famille.* (a place)

*Cet étudiant <u>vit</u> **en** famille.* (It means how, not where)

(*This student lives **with** a family*).

A lifestyle, a manner of being, in parallel with dorm-living (***en** résidence universitaire*; also to designate a place, ***dans** une résidence universitaire*).

Note: The prepositions *in* and *at* are related to manner.

***dans** une guerre* - ***In** a war*

*Ce pays est **en** guerre.* - *This country is **at** war.*

*Le navire est **en** mer.* - *The ship is **at** sea.*

*Enfants **en** **train de** jouer.* - *Children **at** play.*

All the prepositions ***en*** in all the above examples express some manner of being or doing.

IV. <u>ABOUT as a preposition of approximation:</u>

1) <u>in number</u>:

*Ils étaient **environ** / **à peu près** une douzaine.* - *They were **about** a dozen.*

2) <u>of a point in time</u> (a date or time of day):

***vers** le 19 mai* - ***about** May 19*

***vers** 17 heures* - ***about** 5 PM*

3) <u>of a length of time</u>:

*Il est venu pour **environ** un mois.* - *He came for **about** a month.*

4) <u>of a point in space</u>:

*Regardez **autour de** vous.* - *Look **about** (**around**) you.*

*Des papiers traînaient **partout**.* - Papers were lying **about**.

V. *ON* and its various relations.

Note: The equivalent uses of this preposition show particularly well the relativity of perception of common realities between languages.

1) **date**:

J'arriverai vendredi. (no preposition) - *I will arrive **on** Friday.*

J'arriverai le 22 mai. (no preposition) - *I will arrive **on** May 22.*

2) **place**:

*Mettez le document **sur** le bureau.* - Put the book **on** the desk.

*travailler **à** la ferme/**dans** une ferme* - to work **on** the farm

*marcher **dans** la rue* - to walk **on** the street

3) **with a gerund**:

*Elle a souri **en** me voyant.* - She smiled **upon** seeing me.

4) **theme/topic**:

*Un livre **sur** la Chine.* - A book **on** China.

5) **vehicles and movement**:

dans** l'avion/le bus/le* train (sur*** would be quite dangerous!) - **on** the plane/bus/train to travel **on** foot, **on** horseback   *voyager **à** pied, **à** cheval*

VI. *TO* and its various relations:

1) **Place**:

a) with a verb: *Je suis allé **à** Chicago.* - I went **to** Chicago.

b) object of a noun:

*l'avion **à destination de** Chicago - the plane **to** Chicago*

Note: This last case is explained in the next section: "Amplification of a preposition."

2) **Place with names of countries**:

Although the system is fairly simple, errors keep coming back among students with prepositions and articles for names of countries. This is probably due to the deep-rooted habit in naming countries in English, distinguishing between static and dynamic situations.

Compare:

*We live **in** France.* (static)

*We go **to** France.* (dynamic)

With names of countries, French does not differentiate between static and dynamic situations, and instead treats names of countries according to their gender or initial letter.

*Nous vivons **en** France.* (feminine)

*Nous allons **en** France.* (feminine)

*Nous vivons **au** Canada.* (masculine)

*Nous allons **au** Canada.* (masculine)

Nous vivons **en** Israël.

Nous allons **en** Israël.

Gender is irrelevant when a masculine country begins with a vowel. Compare the two states below that are masculine:

au Nouveau-Mexique, *but* **en** Arizona

3) **Place with names of islands**:

16th century France probably distinguished between distant, unexplored islands as viewed on a rudimentary world map and very familiar islands of Europe. And this old usage remained in the language:

a) **Distant islands** viewed as dots or spots on such maps: **à** Cuba, **à** Madagascar, **à** la/en Martinique, **à** Tahiti, etc.

b) **Nearby islands**: viewed as familiar larger space (in more detailed European maps): *en* Corse, *en* Sardaigne, *en* Sicile, etc.

Note: *En Martinique* is more modern, since Martinique became a French province (département) in the 1940s.

4) **Moral relation**:

*Soyez polis **envers** vos parents.* - *Be polite **to** your parents.*

*Soyez bons **pour/envers** les animaux.* - *Be kind **to** animals.*

VII. Amplification of a preposition:

French prepositions *à* and *de*, due to their many uses and meanings over time, appear to have lost much of the original semantic force and dynamism that their English equivalents have preserved. This is also the case with other French prepositions, but to a lesser extent (as we shall see).

Perhaps this situation is due to a difference in point of view: While English tends to view actions in their unraveling, French often project them in their state of completion, as a done deal.

Examples:

*J'aime **la lecture**.* (action as a whole and static; though *lire* is also possible) - *I enjoy **reading**.* (action in its progression).

*Moi, j'**aime** ça !* (there is no way here to stress progression) - *I am **liking** it!*

*J'aime **la peinture** à l'huile.* (action is expressed as a single static act) - *I like **painting** with oils.*

Often, French prepositions need to be ***amplified*** in some way to regain this dynamism:

1) <u>using a prepositional phrase or a semantic precision</u>:

De la part de *Jim* (*de* alone would be insufficient) - (On a gift) ***From*** *Jim*

Pour** Ann* (*de* would be insufficient; and ***pour is more dynamic than *à*) - ***To** Ann*

From:/ Expéditeur: / To: / Destinataire: (Precise nouns are more dynamic than short overused prepositions!) - (On a package) ***From***:

2) by <u>a relative clause, more dynamic</u>:

*le monde **qui** nous **entoure*** - *the world **around** us*

*le chemin **qui mène** au lac* - *the path **to** the lake*

*l'amitié **qu'il a pour** vous* - *his friendship **for** you*

3) by <u>a participle</u>:

*un panneau **portant** ces mots* - *a board **with** these words*

*un coup de feu **parti de** la maison* - *a gunshot shot **from** the house*

4) by <u>an infinitive, more dynamic</u>:

*J'ai envoyé **chercher** le médecin.* - *I sent **for** the doctor.*

*Il est sorti **(pour) prendre** une bière.* - *He went out **for** a beer.*

*Aide-moi **à sortir** d'ici !* - *Help me **out** of here!*

Côte à Côte 2

EXERCISES

1. Complete the following text with prepositions. Provide articles as needed.

This text is an excerpt from Antoine de Saint-Exupéry's tale, <u>Le Petit Prince</u>.

J'ai ainsi vécu seul, (without) _____ personne avec qui parler véritablement, (until) _____ une panne dans le désert du Sahara, _____ six ans (ago). Quelque chose s'était cassé (in) _____ mon moteur. Et comme je n'avais (with) _____ moi ni mécanicien, ni passagers, je me préparai _____ essayer de réussir, tout seul, une réparation difficile. C'était (for) _____ moi une question de vie ou de mort. J'avais à peine de l'eau _____ boire (for) _____ huit jours.

Le premier soir je me suis donc endormi sur le sable (a thousand miles away from) _____ toute terre habitée. J'étais bien plus isolé qu'un naufragé sur un radeau (in the middle of) _____ l'Océan. Alors vous imaginez ma surprise, (at day break), _____ quand une drôle de petite voix m'a réveillé. Elle disait :

– S'il vous plaît... dessine-moi un mouton ! – Hein !
– Dessine-moi un mouton...

J'ai sauté sur mes pieds comme si j'avais été frappé (by) _____ la foudre. J'ai bien frotté mes yeux. J'ai bien regardé. Et j'ai vu un petit bonhomme tout à fait extraordinaire qui me considérait gravement. Voilà le meilleur portrait que, plus tard, je (managed to) _____ faire de lui. Mais mon dessin, bien sûr, est beaucoup moins ravissant que le modèle. Ce n'est pas ma faute. J'avais été découragé dans ma carrière _____ peintre (by) _____ les grandes personnes, à l'âge de six ans, et je n'avais rien appris (to draw) _____, sauf les boas fermés et les boas ouverts.

Je regardai donc cette apparition avec des yeux tout ronds (with) _____ étonnement. N'oubliez pas que je me trouvais (a thousand miles away from) _____ de toute région habitée. Or mon petit bonhomme ne me semblait ni égaré, ni (dead tired) _____, ni (starved to death) _____, ni (dying of thirst) _____ , ni (scared to death) _____. Il n'avait en rien l'apparence d'un enfant perdu au milieu du désert, (a thousand miles from) _____ de toute région habitée. **Change this to:**

(Excerpt from LE PETIT PRINCE by Antoine de Saint-Exupéry. Copyright 1943 by Houghton Mifflin Harcourt Publishing Company. Copyright© renewed 1971 by Consuelo de Saint-Exupéry. Reprinted by permission of Houghton Mifflin Harcourt Publishing Company. All rights reserved.).

2. Complete the following texts with prepositions of time and place:

1) Ma chère maman,

Je suis bien arrivé _____ Paris ce matin (three hours ago) _____. A l'aéroport, il m'a fallu attendre (for) _____ au moins une heure (before) _____ prendre le car d'Air France (up to) _____ centre de la ville. (I have been in) _____ à mon hôtel (for) _____ environ une heure. Je reste à Paris (for) _____ quelques jours, (until) _____dimanche. (In) _____ quelques jours donc, je prendrai alors un train qui me mènera (to) _____ Angers, (in) _____ deux heures de temps.

Je te téléphonerai (in) _____ une semaine, pour te donner de mes nouvelles et te parler de mes cours (at) _____ l'université.

Je t'embrasse, Jimmy

2) Il a vécu en Afrique _____ deux ans dans le cadre des Peace Corps. C'était _____ dix ans, et il n'y est pas retourné (since) _____.

3) J'étais venu à Angers (for) _____ un an, mais j'ai fini par m'y établir. Et _____ bientôt dix ans que j'y habite. Peut-être même suis-je ici (for) _____ le restant de mes jours !

3. Supply the proper preposition for each following verbs. And provide any article as needed: (You may add to the lists).

1. **Nous allons:** *France, Canada, Colombie, Madagascar, Antilles, Nouvelle-Orléans, Cuba, Névada, Arizona, banlieue, Martinique, Colorado, Chicago, etc.*

2. **Nous habitons:** *France, Canada, Colombie, Madagascar, Antilles, Nouvelle-Orléans, Cuba, Névada, Arizona, banlieue, Martinique, Colorado, Chicago, etc.*

4. Complete the following sentences with the French equivalents of a selection of English prepositions: *about, from, in, on, to.*

1. Quand pouvez-vous commencer le travail ? -- Je puis commencer (in) _____ une semaine. -- Et combien de temps vous faut-il pour le terminer ? -- Je puis tout faire (in) _____ trois jours.

2. Préférez-vous vivre (in) _____ famille ou (in) _____ résidence universitaire ? (two solutions)

3. (In) _____ cette manière, on a plus de chance de réussir.

4. Le magasin n'est pas ouvert (on Sundays) _____ .

5. Elle est tombée (in) _____ descendant l'escalier.

6. Nous nous sommes rencontrés (on) _____ le train (to) _____ Dijon.

7. Est-ce que l'avion de Denver est déjà arrivé à la porte d'embarquement ? -- L'avion (from) _____ Denver ou celui (to) _____ Denver ?

8. Il faut (about) _____ trois heures pour ce vol. Comme nous avons décollé (at about) _____ midi, nous devrions atterrir (in) _____ une vingtaine de minutes.

5. Translate the following sentences, amplifying the prepositions as needed.

Examples:

I received an email *from* Paul for Mary

J'ai reçu un courriel *de* Paul pour Marie.

(No amplification needed with a dynamic verb: *j'ai reçu*)

(But on a gift) **From** Jim **De la part de** Jim **To** Ann **Pour** Ann

Jacques Bourgeacq

(Amplification needed for lack of stated dynamic verb)

1. I helped the elderly lady who lives <u>across</u> the street.

2. The sentences <u>in</u> this exercise are simple.

3. The people <u>with</u> her come <u>from</u> France.

4. The guy <u>next to</u> me <u>on</u> the plane was snoring!

5. I helped the elderly lady <u>across</u> the street.

6. I got this job <u>through</u> him.

7. In France, you can still <u>send for</u> a doctor.

8. We heard a shot coming <u>from</u> the house.

9. The world <u>around</u> us is still mysterious.

10. We'll all end up six feet <u>under</u>!

Chapter 15

The rich and varied world of adverbs

Le monde riche et varié des adverbes

As its name indicates, an **adverb** (**ad** + **verb** = *toward, next to the verb*) is a word (most often invariable in form) or a phrase, that modifies a verb, an adjective, another adverb, or even a whole sentence.

Examples:

Parlez **lentement**.

Parlez **plus lentement**. (*plus* modifies the adverb *lentement*)

Il a un accent **très** *prononcé*. (*très* modifies the adjective *prononcé*)

Evidemment, *il parle avec un accent*. (modifies the whole sentence)

Both English and French have a vast number of adverbs and phrases that perform the adverbial (i.e. circumstantial) function. They play a similar role for verbs as adjectives play for nouns. Along with prepositions and conjunctions, adverbs place an action into a certain circumstance (time, place, manner, cause, probability, affirmation, negation, etc.).

Although with some degree of syntactic mobility (for emphasis), French adverbs tend to follow the verb, but usually precede adjectives and other adverbs.

Adverbs are too numerous for a comprehensive review in this book. Most of them can be viewed as vocabulary and learned best by sheer memory, as they have exact equivalents in English: ***toujours*** (always, still), ***demain*** (tomorrow), ***ici*** (here), ***loin*** (far), etc. The same applies to adverbial phrases: ***avant-hier*** (the day before yesterday), ***après-demain*** (the day after tomorrow), ***d'ici là*** (by now, by then), ***tôt ou tard*** (sooner or later), ***mal à propos*** (inappropriately), ***tout-à-coup*** (all of a sudden), etc.

There are cases, however, that do need a second look:

1) Correspondence of adverbs of time:

Adverbs of time can vary according to the perspective:

present perspective	past or future perspective
avant-hier	*l'avant-veille*
hier	*la veille*
aujourd'hui	*ce jour-là*
demain	*le lendemain*
après-demain	*le surlendemain*
ce matin	*ce matin-là*
le semestre dernier	*le semestre suivant*

Examples:

*Je **sais** qu'il arrivera **après-demain**.* (present perspective)

*Je **savais** qu'il arriverait **le surlendemain**.* (past perspective)

*Je **saurai** demain s'il arrivera **ce jour-là**.* (future perspective)

2) Correspondence adverb/adjective as comparative and superlative words:

	Positive	Comparative	Superlative
adjective:	bon	meilleur	le meilleur
	mauvais	pire, plus mauvais	le pire, le plus mauvais
	petit	plus petit, moindre	le plus petit, le moindre

	Positive	Comparative	Superlative
adverb:	bien	mieux	le mieux
	mal	pire, plus mal	le pire, le plus mal
	peu	moins	le moins
	beaucoup	plus, davantage	le plus

Examples:

*Entre deux maux, il faut choisir **le moindre**.* - Between two evils, choose **the lesser**.

*Il travaille **beaucoup**, mais je travaille **davantage**/**plus que lui**.* - He works **a lot**, but I work **even more**.

*Tu dis que ce chanteur est **meilleur**; moi, je trouve que l'autre chante **mieux**.* (English does not distinguish between adjective and adverb in the case of *better*: here lies the source of the confusion)

Note on the origin: Latin masculine/feminine word *melior* --> *meilleur*. Latin neuter *melius* --> *mieux*. *Melior* became the French adjective, while *melius* became the adverb. This is perhaps an arbitrary choice, although the neuter gender points to an adverb, rather than an adjective.

3) The equivalents of the English adverb *late*:

Examples:

*Il est **tard**, je sais ! Et je suis **en retard** parce que le train avait **du retard**. Et **dernièrement** il y a moins de trains. En outre, je n'avais pas vu que **ma montre retardait**.*

It is **late**, I know! And I am **late** because the train was **late**. And **lately** there are fewer trains. Also I had not seen that my **watch** was **slow**.

Note: My watch is **fast**. --> Ma montre **avance**.

4) **Double nature and function of some adverbs:**

As if not complicated enough, English adverbs can also be adjectives! A fairly large number of such words can be both adjectives or adverbs: **late, early, slow, fast, weekly, daily, low, high, good, bad,** etc.

Examples:

Le **dernier** numéro de ce magazine - The **late** issue of this magazine (adjective)

--Do you receive this magazine **weekly**? (adverb)

--Yes, it is a **weekly** magazine. (adjective)

I hear you **loud** and **clear**! (instead of *loudly* and *clearly*)

This cheese smells **bad** but tastes **good**. (adverbs)

Though this situation exists also in French, there are relatively fewer French adjectives that can be used as adverbs. Here are some examples: **bon, mauvais, fort, cher, bas, droit** and **haut**:

Ce parfum ne sent pas **bon** mais coûte **cher** !

Ces oiseaux volent **bas**.

Parle plus **fort**, je t'entends mal.

Avec la discipline militaire, on doit marcher **droit** !

5) The derivation of adjectives into adverbs:

Over time, both English and French have coined many new words, usually by adding a *prefix* or a *suffix*. This process allows the meaning of a word to be adapted to another function in a sentence: e.g. from verb to noun, from adjective to adverb, etc.

Examples of derivation:

*traduire --> tradu**it**, tradu**ction** --> tradu**cteur**, tradu**ctrice***

*réel --> réal**ité** --> réal**iser** --> **ir**réel --> réel**lement**,* etc.

In both languages, one of the most productive derivations has been from adjective to adverb, by adding a suffix: *--ly* in English and *--ment* in French.

The English suffix *--ly* comes from old English **lich**, meaning *form, body, shape, appearance*. The adverb **like** is of the same root.

Similarly, the French suffix *--ment* comes from Latin and old French: **mens/mentis**, meaning *mind, mental process*. So the word **gentiment**, for example, can be understood as *"in a spirit of gentleness"* or *"mindfully gentle."* But of course, it corresponds idiomatically to **gently** or **kindly** in English.

The ease of coining an adverb from an adjective has created a vast number of such adverbs in French, and they tend to produce a heavy-handed style (lengthy words) when used profusely on a page. These adverbs have given rise to alternate adverbial phrases (*locutions adverbiales*) that can advantageously replace a heavy, lengthy adverb. Also, a noun (called also a *substantive*) mentally carries more weight than an adverb.

Examples:

*Agir audacieuse**ment** --> agir **avec** audace*

*Travailler courageuse**ment** --> travailler **avec** courage*

Ils vivent harmonieusement --> *Ils vivent **en** harmonie*

Agir inconsidérément --> *agir **de façon** inconsidérée*

6) From adjective to adverb: Expressions of place:

The rich system of adverbs of place needs some review: the prepositions *sur, sous,* and *dans* have produced corresponding adverbs:

Latin *sursum* --> *sur* --> *de + sursum* --> *dessus* --> *au-dessus* --> *par-dessus* --> *là-dessus,*

Latin *subtus* --> *sous* --> *de + subtus* --> *dessous* --> *au-dessous* --> *par-dessous* --> *là-dessous*

Latin *de + intus* (from within) --> *dans* --> *dedans* --> *au-dedans* -> *là- dedans*

Examples:

*L'enveloppe est-elle **sur** le buffet ? --Oui, elle est **dessus.***

*Un timbre est collé **dessus** (sur) l'enveloppe.* (preposition or adverb)

*Cette famille habite (à l'étage) **au-dessus**.* (preposition or adverb)

*Le chien a sauté **par-dessus** le mur.* (preposition of movement: = over)

*Cette valise est-elle pleine ? --Non, il n'y a presque rien **dedans**.* (inside)

7) Formation of adverbs ending in --ment:

a) With many adjectives, *--ment* is added to their feminine form, probably due to the ease of pronunciation of the vowel ending:

capricieux --> *capricieuse* --> *capricieusement*

b) With adjectives ending in --*ent* or --*ant*, the consonnant *m* of the ending is doubled:

abondant --> *abondamment* (abundantly)

étonnant --> *étonnamment* (astonishingly)

récent --> *récemment* (recently)

évident --> *évidemment* (evidently)

Note: The *e* of these --*emment* adverbs is pronounced as *a*.

8) The adverbs of negation: Types and place.

a) **Types**: At the end of Chapter 5, the negation *ne* was discussed in connection with words (nouns, pronouns, adverbs) forming negative adverbial phrases: ***ne***... *personne, rien, aucun, pas, point, plus, jamais*. But when used alone, these words were historically positive, and some of them still are so today. They became negative only from their long and frequent association with the negation *ne*.

Examples:

*Avez-vous **jamais** vu un tel spectacle ?* (Without *ne*, the word *jamais* means *ever*, rather than *never*)

Note: ***Jamais*** is an old French combination of *ja* + *magis* (i.e. *now* + *more*). The same root is found in the conjunction ***mais*** in French.

A similar process is found in English with the words ***ever*** and ***never*** (*not ever*). We can recognize *ja* (*now*) as part of ***déjà*** (*already*).

b) **Place**: First of all, unlike the English avoidance of double or triple negations, French readily accumulates them.

He **never** said <u>anything</u> <u>more</u> to <u>any</u>one.

*Il n'a **plus jamais rien** dit à **personne**.*

OR:

Il n'a jamais plus rien dit à personne.

Note: In fact, if we consider that these words are **pseudo-negations**, the reason for their accumulation as double and triple negatives (a "no-no" in English!) should come much less as a surprise!

One more remark about their place in the sentence: As direct object (*rien*) and indirect object (*à personne*), they have priority next to the verb (*a dit*), while *à personne* comes after, due to its length and as a matter of sentence rhythm. The other negations, purely adverbial, are pushed aside in whichever order.

c) **Place of the negations with an infinitive**:

To negate an infinitive, the adverbial phrases *ne + pas, ne + jamais, ne + point, ne + plu*s, etc., are usually linked together and placed before the verb (except *personne*).

Examples:

*Il m'a dit de **ne plus rien** dire à **personne**.* - He told me **not** to say **anything more** to **anyone**.

*Il m'a demandé de **ne jamais plus** lui en parler.* - He asked me **never** to talk to him about it **again**.

OR:

*Il m'a demandé de **ne plus jamais** lui en parler.*

EXERCISES

1. In the following list, select the adverbs or adverbial phrases that are suitable for each context.

autrefois, de nos jours, dorénavant, jadis, jusqu'ici, n'importe où, partout, pour l'instant, pour le moment, parfois, prochainement, récemment.

Examples:

Nous aurons pris une décision <u>entre maintenant et cette date</u>.

*Nous aurons pris une décision **d'ici là** (or **entretemps**).*

<u>A partir de maintenant</u>, faites plus attention !

***Dorénavant** (**Désormais**), faites plus attention !*

1. La situation évolue rapidement. On constate <u>depuis quelque temps</u> certains changements inquiétants.

2. Nous n'avons pas pu <u>jusqu'à maintenant</u> donner suite à votre demande. Mais nous vous promettons qu'<u>à partir d'</u>aujourd'hui nous sommes en mesure de considérer votre candidature. Vous aurez de nos nouvelles <u>très bientôt</u>.

3. Nous n'avons pas ce produit en stock <u>maintenant</u>, mais nous en avons commandé et attendons <u>bientôt</u> un arrivage.

4. Je me demande si <u>avant</u> on vivait plus en sécurité qu'<u>aujourd'hui</u>.

5. <u>Quelquefois</u> j'ai l'impression que les gens n'écoutent pas ce qu'on leur dit !

6. On trouve ce produit <u>dans tous les endroits</u>.

7. J'irais <u>à quelque endroit que ce soit</u> pour avoir un bon job.

2. Transpose the following text into a past perspective. Make all necessary changes: adverbes and verb tenses.

Example:

<u>*Ce matin*</u> *j'ai décidé...* --> ***Ce matin-là** j'avais décidé...*

Ce matin j'ai décidé en me levant qu'*aujourd'hui* ne sera pas un jour comme les autres. Et comme je n'ai pas fait la fête *hier soir*, je crois pouvoir rester éveillé *jusqu'à ce soir* sans trop de difficulté. Je dois donc profiter de ces heureuses circonstances pour commencer à travailler à ces deux devoirs qu'il me faudra remettre *la semaine prochaine* à mes deux professeurs de littérature. Je sais que je m'y prends un peu tard, que j'aurais dû commencer mes recherches *il y a trois semaines*... mais on ne fait pas toujours ce qu'on veut et je saurai bien me débrouiller, comme *au semestre dernier*.

3. Same exercise as 2: Rewrite from a past perspective. Begin with: *C'était ce jour-là un mercredi...*

C'est *aujourd'hui* mercredi et j'ai reçu *avant-hier* un courriel de mes parents qui m'annoncent leur visite pour *après-demain* vendredi. Malgré tout l'amour filial et le respect que j'éprouve à leur égard, et le plaisir que j'aurais *en ce moment* à les voir, cette visite ne pourrait venir à un plus mauvais moment : je dois achever *dans une semaine* un long devoir que j'ai commencé *le mois dernier* et qui *jusqu'à maintenant* n'a avancé que péniblement ! Je dois donc *à présent* envoyer un texto à mes parents pour leur demander diplomatiquement de bien vouloir repousser leur visite à *la semaine prochaine*.

4. To improve the style, replace the adverbs ending in --*ment*, with an adverbial phrase: (A dictionary may be useful).

Examples:

Elle danse **gracieusement**.

Elle danse **avec grâce**.

Le projet a été voté **immédiatement**.

Le projet a été voté **sur-le-champ**. (= right off the bat)

1. Ne vous engagez pas légèrement.

2. Ils s'aiment follement.

3. Il a débarqué chez nous inopinément.

4. Cette terre produit abondamment.

5. Elle a fait sa valise hâtivement.

6. Ne prenez pas littéralement tout ce qu'on vous dit.

7. Une langue s'apprend graduellement et patiemment.

8. Ce professeur distribue les mauvaises notes impitoyablement.

9. Il mérite incontestablement le premier prix.

10. Est-ce qu'on pourrait passer cette soirée paisiblement ?

11. Nous l'avons cherché vainement.

12. En entendant ce bruit, il s'est retourné soudainement.

5. Insert the adverbs in the proper place in each sentence:

Examples:

(souvent, pas) *On ne le voit prendre de risques...*

*On ne le voit **pas souvent** prendre de risques.*

(A peine) *Il était sorti, quand on le demanda au téléphone.*

*Il était **à peine** sorti, quand on le demanda au téléphone.*

***A peine était-il sorti** qu'on le demanda au téléphone.*

(Note the construction when *A peine* is emphasized; note also that *Aussi* means *therefore* when placed at the beginning of a sentence).

1. (quelque part/déjà) -- J'ai l'impression de vous avoir rencontré
   (nulle part/jamais) -- Vous faites erreur, je ne vais...

2. (maintenant/partout/même) On le voit dans les cercles littéraires de la capitale.

3. (jamais, rien, de pareil) Avez-vous vu...

4. (aussi = therefore; use interrogative construction) Elle voulait arriver plus vite... Elle a pris l'avion.

5. (peut-être) Il aura oublié notre rendez-vous.

6. (inlassablement) Il a travaillé toute sa vie.....

7. (jamais/plus/ailleurs/nulle part) Il a disparu d'ici; et on ne l'a revu...

8. (pas/trop/tout de même) Tu ne vas me reprocher de t'avoir aidé !

6. Comparative and superlative adverbs and adjectives. Translate the following sentences to highlight the difference.

Examples:

*C'est le **meilleur** étudiant **de** notre classe.* - He is the **best** student **in** our class. (adjective)

*Oui, c'est lui qui travaille **le mieux**.* - Yes, he is the one who works **best**. (adverb)

1. He sings well, but she dances better than he does.

2. I play tennis fairly well, but less spectacularly than Sally.

3. My grades are not so bad, but not as good as yours.

4. The more I taste it, the more I like it.

5. Most of my friends are as weak as I am in math.

6. One must choose the lesser of two evils.

7. She is at least as smart as her older sister.

8. The more the merrier. (A proverb. Consult the dictionary)

9. The economy is worse this year than last year.

10. I spend much less than my brother, but I also save a little more.

11. Mount Everest is one of the highest mountains in the world.

12. It is she who earns the least money.

Jacques Bourgeacq

Chapter 16

The syntax of emphasis

Syntaxe de la mise en relief

English and French differ in the manner in which an element in a sentence is emphasized. English often tends to leave the order of words unchanged, while stressing vocally or highlighting visually the element to be emphasized. French, on the other hand, resorts to deviations from its normal order of words, either by repetition and/or by dislocation of this element. Each language has its own of strategy designed to give special importance and draw attention to a particular element of the message.

I. **Repetition in French for plain emphasis.**

An element is repeated or displaced for emphasis.

Examples:

Ce livre, je l'***ai lu***. (et non pas seulement feuilleté ou remarqué) - I have **read** this book. (I did not just leaf through it, or heard about it)

Moi, j'ai lu ce livre. (moi, parmi d'autres personnes) - ***I*** have read this book. (I for one have read it)

Je ***l'***ai lu, ***ce livre***. (ce livre en particulier, parmi d'autres possibles) - I have read ***this book***. (this specific book, among others)

<u>Note</u>: While these French constructions are not foreign to the English language, they are not nearly as frequent.

II. <u>Dislocation in French for exclusive emphasis:</u>

French distinguishes between plain emphasis and <u>*exclusive (i.e. selective)*</u> emphasis. *Highlighting or selecting, that is the question?* In Chapter 4, (III, Demonstrative pronouns, "A problematic case"), we had begun discussing ***c'est*** and ***il est*** as devices for presenting or emphasizing an action: ***il est*** as an <u>impersonal</u> formula <u>introducing</u> an action and ***c'est*** as <u>recapitulating</u> it.

In addition, ***C'est...qui/ C'est ...que*** serve as <u>selective</u> devices:

1. *C'est... qui* presents an element, <u>subject</u> of the verb, as *exclusive* or *unique*. A couple of examples will clearly show this distinction between *plain* emphasis and *exclusive or selective* emphasis:

*Qui a lu <u>Le Petit Prince</u>? -- **Moi, je** l'ai lu.* (plain emphasis = I for one; I among other readers; no exclusivity here). - *Who has read <u>The Little Prince</u>? -- **I** have read it.*

Qui a écrit Le Petit Prince? ***C'est*** *Antoine de Saint-Exupéry **qui** l'a écrit.* (exclusive emphasis: it is he who wrote it, and nobody else). - *Who wrote <u>The Little Prince</u>? -- <u>Antoine de Saint-Exupéry</u> wrote it.* (no change in English in the syntax; emphasis vocally or visually).

<u>Note</u>: Seldom stated in French textbooks, a sentence like *"Antoine de Saint-Exupéry l'a écrit"* <u>cannot</u> be an answer to the question "Who wrote it," since an author is usually known to be the <u>exclusive</u> performer of that action. The same would apply to *"Qui a découvert l'Amérique?"*. The reply would necessarily need the device ***C'est ... qui***, since an <u>exclusive</u> performer of the action is expected to be the answer. In contrast, with the sentence *"**Qu'est que** Saint-Exupéry a écrit?"* the answer can be: "***Saint-Exupéry*** (or simply *Il*) *a écrit <u>Le Petit Prince</u>*," since no exclusivity, nor even emphasis, is felt in this instance.

   1. ***C'est... que***, can introduce an element of the sentence whose function is <u>object</u> of the verb or is <u>adverbial,</u> if an exclusivity is felt.

Example:

C'est <u>Le Petit Prince</u> *que nous avons lu.* (ce n'est pas un autre livre) - We have read <u>The Little Prince</u>. (implying, with emphasis, that we are referring to that book only)

Note: **Le Petit Prince**, *nous l'avons lu.*, would be a mere emphasis, simply meaning "Speaking of that book, we did read it."

Another example:

C'est <u>avec plaisir</u> *que nous acceptons votre invitation.* - We accept your invitation <u>with pleasure</u>. (vocal emphasis)

Note: Without emphasis, the French sentence would simply be: "*Nous acceptons votre invitation avec plaisir.*"

3. *Il y a ... qui/ Il y a ... que* can be used to emphasize the existence or presence of an element, especially when it is naturally vague in content or unspecified.

Examples:

Quelqu'un est venu vous voir.

Il y a quelqu'un <u>qui</u> est venu vous voir. (emphasized)

(Someone came to see you.)

Il y a <u>des choses</u> qu'il vaut mieux ne pas dire. (Some things are better left unsaid.)

4. *Il y a ...que / Voilà ... que/ Cela fait ... que* can be used to emphasize an adverbial element of <u>time</u>. These devices replace **depuis**.

Examples:

*Nous habitons dans cette ville **depuis trois ans**.*

Il y a <u>trois ans</u> **que** *nous habitons dans cette ville.*

Voilà <u>trois ans</u> **que** *nous habitons dans cette ville.*

Cela fait *trois ans* **que** *nous habitons dans cette ville.*

EXERCISES

1. Identify the emphasis in the following sentences, and re-establish the basic, unstressed sentence.

<u>Example:</u>

<u>Ce sont</u> *les lapins* **<u>qui</u>** *ont été étonnés!* (Alphonse Daudet)

Les lapins ont été étonnés. (***ce sont... qui***: exclusive, selective emphasis: only the rabbits or mainly the rabbits)

1. Mais qu'est-ce qu'on leur a fait à mes chèvres? (Daudet)

2. C'est à moi qu'il appartient de dire la vérité. (Voltaire)

3. Maurice les aimait tant les cerises. (Daudet)

4. C'est par orgueil que nous sommes polis. (Montesquieu)

5. Les chèvres, il leur faut du large. (Daudet)

6. Il me plaît beaucoup ce tableau.

7. C'est à moi que vous osez parler ainsi?

8. C'est en forgeant qu'on devient forgeron. (proverb)

9. Vaste, cette maison l'était!

10. Apprendre une langue, ce n'est pas très facile.

2. Emphasize the underlined element, using a simple or an exclusive option as applicable.

Examples:

Une nouvelle vie commence.

C'est une nouvelle vie qui commence. (exclusive)

Ce vin est délicieux!

Il est délicieux, ce vin! (plain emphasis)

1. Cette maison était vaste.

2. Agir ainsi est honteux.

3. On n'obtient pas un diplôme sans effort.

4. Maintenant il faut faire attention.

5. On doit le respect à ses parents. (two solutions)

6. Je suis né dans cette petite ville.

7. J'habite dans ce pays depuis longtemps.

8. On voit le maçon au pied du mur. (proverb)

9. La même erreur revient à chaque fois.

10. Comme ce paysage est beau!

11. Je veux la tranquillité. (double emphasis)

12 J'ai économisé cet argent pour mes enfants.

3. Answer these questions with a complete sentence, with a form of emphasis

Examples:

Qui a découvert l'Amérique? (les Vikings)

Ce sont *les Vikings* **qui** *ont découvert l'Amérique.*

Ce sont *les Vikings* **qui** *l'ont découverte.*

Et vous, avez-vous visité ce musée? (oui)

Oui, **moi, je** *l'ai déjà visité.*

1. Qu'est-ce qui a développé la littérature? (l'invention de l'imprimerie)

2. Quel est votre héros favori? (....)

3. Depuis combien de temps êtes-vous à l'université? (six mois)

4. Etes-vous déjà allé en Europe? (non) (emphasize three elements in three separate replies)

5. Vas-tu souvent à la piscine? (oui) (+ double emphasis in one reply)

6. Que voulez-vous donc? (la justice + double emphasis)

7. Pourquoi avez-vous volé ce pain? (avoir faim)

8. Paul n'a pas apporté ce cadeau; son frère l'a apporté. (double emphasis)

4. Translate the following sentences, emphasizing the underlined elements in the English text.

Example:

<u>I</u> hate **<u>spinach</u>**! (double emphasis)

Moi, <u>*les épinards*</u>, *je déteste ça!*

1. I have been waiting <u>for three hours</u>.

2. I am talking <u>to you</u>.

3. I brought these flowers <u>for you</u>.

4. Who wrote this poem? -- <u>I</u> wrote it.

5. <u>Some people</u> are dishonest.

6. <u>Who</u> told you that?

7. <u>Some things</u> are not clear in this contract.

8. <u>I</u> called you, <u>it was not</u> my roommate. (double emphasis)

9. <u>I</u> would never do such a thing.

10. <u>To leave</u> is to die a little.

11. <u>I</u> like <u>chocolate</u>. (double emphasis)

12. We have been waiting <u>for one hour</u>.

Jacques Bourgeacq

Glossary of grammatical terms:

ADJECTIVE (un adjectif): *A word modifying a noun.*

- qualifying (qualificatif): Adding a quality or characteristic.

- adjectival phrase (locution adjectivale): A phrase functioning as an adjective.

- demonstrative (démonstratif) : Indefinite (indéfini); interrogative (interrogatif).

- possessive (possessif): Showing ownership. Not to be confused with pronouns of the same category.

ADVERB (un adverbe): *A word modifying a verb, another adverb or an adjective.*

- adverbial phrase (locution adverbiale): A word unit functioning as an adverb.

AGREEMENT (un accord): *Conformity of form between two or more related words.*

- subject/verb (sujet/verbe)

- noun/adjective (nom/adjectif)

- past participle (participe passé): part of a composite verb, sometimes an adjective

ANTECEDENT (un antécédent): *A word referred to by another word: e.g., a <u>relative</u> pronoun repeating and standing for a preceding noun or pronoun.*

ARTICLE (un article): *A particle presenting a noun in a certain light.*

- definite (défini): Presented as specific or general.

- indefinite (indéfini): Presented as one or more of a series.

- partitive (partitif): Presented as part of a whole category.

CLAUSE (une proposition): *A part of a sentence, containing a conjugated verb.*

- main or leading (principale): The clause on which one or several clauses depend.

- independent (indépendante): One sentence without any dependent clause.

- coordinate (coordonnée): One of two or more connected independent clauses.

- subordinate (subordonnée): A clause attached to, and dependent on, a main clause.

CONJUNCTION (une conjonction): *A word or phrase introducing a clause.*

- subordinate (subordonnée): Depending on, and adding a circumstance or characteristic to a main clause.

- coordinate (coordonnée): Uniting two independent clauses in a parallel relationship.

DERIVATION (une dérivation): *Construction of a word from a basic root (e.g., franc --> franchement).*

FUNCTION (une fonction): *The role played by a word or word unit in a sentence.*

- subject (sujet): Word producing an action.

- direct object (objet direct): Word receiving an action directly, without a preposition.

- indirect object (objet indirect): Same as above, but with a preposition, mainly *à*.

- adverbial modifier (locution adverbiale): Adverb or adverbial phrase adding a circumstance to the verb.

- adjectival modifier (locution adjectivale): Same as above, but modifying a noun.

GENDER (un genre) *One of three genders: Feminine, masculine and neuter with their respective forms.*

MOOD (un mode): *The lens through which an action is viewed.*

- indicative (indicatif): Viewed and presented as reality.

- subjunctive (subjonctif): Viewed and presented as subjective thought.

- conditional (conditionnel): Viewed as a condition, or as a thought contrary to fact.

- infinitive (infinitif): A "raw" verb form. The general notion of an action.

- imperative (impératif): The mood of command, ordering.

NUMBER (un nombre): *Applies to nouns, verbs, pronouns, and adjectives, with their respective forms.*

- singular (singulier)

- plural (pluriel)

NOUN (un nom): *A word presenting a thing, person or idea.*

- common (commun): Indicates a thing, idea, as well as a person but in a general sense, as one of a category.

- proper (propre): Indicates a person, country, thing, etc. but as specific or unique. Takes a capital letter as a result.

PHRASE (une proposition, un syntagme): *A part of a sentence or a close unit of words.*

- adjectival phrase (proposition adjectivale; modifies a noun)

- adverbial phrase (proposition adverbiale; modifies a verb)

PREPOSITION (une préposition): *A word that connects other words in a semantic relation.*

- prepositional phrase (locution prépositive): Same as above, but a unit of several words.

PROCESS (un processus): *A role or function performed by a word, phrase or sentence.*

- to modify (modifier): General term. To add a detail that changes the meaning of a word or an action.

- to characterize (caractériser): To add a detail to a noun or a verb that modifies its meaning.

- to particularize (particulariser: To change from general to specific).

- to understate (sous-entendre): To suggest instead of expressing, to imply.

PRONOUN (un pronom) *A word that stands for, and acts as a noun (distinct from an adjective, that accompanies a noun)*

- personal (personnel): Identifies as a person or a thing.

- possessive (possessif): Stands for the possessed noun.

- relative (relatif): Stands for a noun, introducing an adjectival clause.

- demonstrative (démonstratif): Points to, or refers to a noun previously mentioned.

- indefinite (indéfini): a word referring to a noun as a general, vague or an undetermined entity

- interrogative (interrogatif). It stands for a noun in a questioning situation.

SEMANTIC (sémantique): *Refers to the meaning of words* (aside from their function and form).

SENTENCE (une phrase): *A group of word including at least a subject (expressed or implied) and a verb* (not to be confused with <u>a phrase</u>).

- affirmative (affirmative): forming a statement.

- interrogative (interrogative): forming a question.

- negative (négative): negating a statement.

SYNTAX (la syntaxe): *The general study or the description of a construction of words in a sentence* (opposite of Semantics, which concerns the meaning of words, not their place).

- syntactical (syntaxique): Adjective pertaining to the combining of words.

- syntagm: A sequence or cluster of words forming a basic unit.

VERB (un verbe): *A word expressing an action (or a state of things).*

- tense (temps): A notion and form indicating the time of an action

- aspect (aspect): A characteristic of a verb in time (a point, a duration, a repetition, etc.)

- perspective (perspective): The point or angle of perception of an action.

- transitive (transitif): Said of a verb that requires an object for its completion.

- intransitive (intransitif): Said of a verb that is self-completing (needs no object).

- pronominal (pronominal): Said of a transitive verb where subject and object are one and the same.

- conjugation (conjugaison): A series of verb endings (*-ai, -as, -a, -ons,* etc.) corresponding to persons (*je, tu, il, nous,* etc.)

VOICE (une voix): *Indicates who or what performs the action.*

- active (active): The subject performs the action.

- passive (passive): The subject is the receiver of the action (via an agent or not).

- pronominal (pronominale): The action is self-performing, leaving out the subject.

- reflexive (réflexive): A pronominal form, where the action returns to the subject.

- reciprocal (réciproque): A pronominal form, where the action is exchanged between several subjects.

Jacques Bourgeacq

Bibliography:

1) <u>Theory</u>:

Lakoff, George, <u>Metaphors we live by</u>, University of Chicago Press, 2003.

Manon, Simone, Comment concevoir les rapports de la pensée et du langage?, PhiloLog: http://www.philolog.fr/presentation-du-chapitre-xi-le-langage/

Rauzduel-Lambourdière, Nicole, Langage, Langue et Culture, http://web.espe-guadeloupe.fr/wp-content/uploads/2015/10/5_Rauzduel-Lambourdie%CC%80re-2007.pdf

Vinay Jean et Darbelnet, John, <u>Stylistique comparée du français et de l'anglais</u>, Didier, 1977.

2) <u>Grammar and textbooks</u>:

Boularès, Michèle et Frérot, Jean-Louis, <u>Grammaire progressive du français</u>, CLE International, 1999.

Bourgeacq, Jacques, <u>Côte à côte: Etude comparative de l'anglais et du français</u>, Virginia Institute Press, 2015.

Fol, Monique and Barrette, Paul, <u>Un Certain Style</u>, Prentice-Hall, 1991.

Katz, Stacey, <u>Contextualized French Grammar</u>, Heinle, 2012.

Limouzy, Pierre and Bourgeacq, Jacques. <u>Manuel de composition française</u>, McGraw-Hill, 1970.

Ollivier, Jacqueline, <u>Grammaire française</u>, Harcourt Brace Jovanovich, 1978

Rochat, Denise, <u>Contrastes: Grammaire du français courant</u>, Pearson, 2009.

Thacker, Mike and d'Angelo, Casimir, <u>Essential French Grammar</u>, Routledge, 2013.

Collective edition, <u>Stylistique et Traduction</u>, Ecole française de Middlebury College, 1951.

3) <u>Articles</u>:

Bourgeacq, Jacques, «De la langue à la tolérance,» <u>The French Review</u>, Vol.XLIV, N°2, Dec. 1970.

Bourgeacq, Jacques, «L'emploi de quelques temps du passé: une méthode,» <u>The French Review</u>, Vol. XLII, N°6, May 1969.

Bourgeacq, Jacques, «Moi, je ou C'est moi qui ?» <u>The French Review</u>, XLIII, N°3, Fev. 1970. 1969.

Other Books

by Virginia Institute Press

Communicative Focus: Teaching Foreign Language on the Basis of the Native Speaker's Communicative Focus, 2nd Edition, Boris Shekhtman – June 2015

Côte à côte 1: Étude comparative de l'anglais et du français (French/English), Jacques Bourgeacq – November 2015

Diagnostic Assessment at the Superior / Distinguished Threshold, Bella Cohen – January 2015

The Gospel of Damascus (Arabic, French and Spanish language fiction), Omar Imady – November 2016

How to Improve Your Foreign Language IMMEDIATELY, 3rd Edition. Foreign Language Communication Tools, Boris Shekhtman – January 2014

Individualized Study Plans for Very Advanced Students of Foreign Language, Betty Lou Leaver – March 2017

Poemas y Laberintos/Poems and Labyrinths (Spanish/English poetry), Idy Linares – May 2015

Sonría y aprenda/Smile and Learn (Spanish/English – reading, comprehension, and vocabulary building), Idy Linares – September 2014

What Works: Helping Students Reach Native-Like Second-Language Competence, 2nd Edition. Rocío Txabarriaga, editor. Authorial collective: Rajai Rasheed Al-Khanji, James Bernhardt, Gerd Brendel, Tseng Tseng Chang, Dan Davidson, Christian Degueldre, Madeline Ehrman, Surendra Gambhir, Jaiying Howard, Frederick Jackson, Cornelius Kubler, Betty Lou Leaver, Maria Lekič, Natalia Lord, Michael Morrissey, Boris Shekhtman, Kenneth Shepard, Svetlana Sibrina – May 2015

Working with Advanced Foreign Language Students, 2nd Edition, Boris Shekhtman – March 2016

www.virginiainstitutepress.com

www.ingramcontent.com/pod-product-compliance
Lightning Source LLC
Chambersburg PA
CBHW032357040426
42451CB00006B/36